MINDFUL
PHILOSOPHY

MICHAEL J SNOW

authorHOUSE®

AuthorHouse™ UK
1663 Liberty Drive
Bloomington, IN 47403 USA
www.authorhouse.co.uk
Phone: 0800.197.4150

Published by AuthorHouse   10/09/2018

ISBN: 978-1-5462-9237-1 (sc)
ISBN: 978-1-5462-9238-8 (hc)
ISBN: 978-1-5462-9236-4 (e)

TABLE OF CONTENTS

Part 1 Mindful Philosophy: The Why

Part 2 Mindful Philosophy: The Where

MINDFUL PHILOSOPHY

MINDFULNESS AND PHILOSOPHY – UNITY WITHIN DIVERSITY

When you sit quiet and watch yourself, all kinds of things may come to the surface. Do nothing about them, don't react to them; as they come, so they will go, by themselves. All that matters is mindfulness, total awareness of oneself, or rather of ones mind.

From "I am That" by Nisargadatta Maharaj.

....

MINDFUL PHILOSOPHY

MINDFULNESS AND PHILOSOPHY – UNITY WITHIN DIVERSITY

"ALL IS ONE" is an oft quoted statement – an apparent explanation of life's conumdrums and quirks, its ups and downs. But is it true? And if so what actually does it mean? This book takes a good look at the notion that in fact the essence of all humanity is spiritual, and that this is something that can be availed by every one of us. We are designed for this realisation, which is the sub stratum of the world's great teachings, whether new or old, east or west, religious or scientific. So, by using *mindfulness* and harnessing the great powers of reason, presence, and love, it is possible for each and every one of us to realise the blissful and free condition that is our true nature and our birthright.

Michael J Snow

DEDICATION

To YOU, the reader, and so to the One Self of All.

ACKNOWLEDGEMENTS

My thanks are due to John DeVal, leader of the School of Philosophy , Cambridge, who has kindly written the forward to this book, and offered encouragement and support along the way. Also to David Stovold who appraised chapters 1 – 4 and provided useful and welcome advice and a perceptive critique, and to Ranko Pinter, who has been of invaluable assistance in putting together chapter 9. I am indebted to my fellow students and travellers on the path of non-duality, and without whose wisdom, guidance and fellowship this book could not exist. And finally, my heartfelt thanks and appreciation to my long suffering and ever patient wife Lyn, who has read every word and without whose love, understanding and support this book would not have been written.

ENDORSEMENTS

If you seek unity, and acknowledge there are many paths up the mountain, this deeply and widely researched book will appeal to , and nourish, the pilgrim in you. I truly enjoyed reading Michael's pragmatic, down-to-earth and comprehensive study of Non-duality - that which unites us: much needed truth in a post-truth world. His use of metaphor, parable and easy way of writing clearly illustrate a totally possible way forward to a peaceful Future, using the Now, when we learn to be awake, honest - and kind.

-Suzie King (Positive Psychology Stress Coach & HSP Monitor)

This timely book eloquently and thoughtfully opens doors to the 'spiritual' seeker who is pursuing an inner enquiry and search for Self and meaning. The reader is invited into the explorations with an ease and accessibility to a depth and breadth of material and resources, skilfully partnering Mindfulness and Philosophy into a living possibility.

Chantek Mary McNeilage - Mindfulness Teacher & Supervisor
www.becomingmindful.co.uk

FOREWORD

Although the title of this book is *Mindful Philosophy* it could equally well have been called *Unity in Diversity*. This is its theme in reviewing the common ground amongst various religious, spiritual and scientific teachings from ancient times to the present day. In this book, Michael Snow prefers to use 'non-duality' to the word 'unity' and this emphasises the fact that duality is normally how we view the world; good and bad, right and wrong, ancient and modern etc. But the most persistent duality is the idea of 'me' and 'the rest of the world' and this is a major barrier in any pursuit of truth because there are a lot of 'me's out there in the rest of the world holding the same idea.

There are also many teachings around and it is an all too common tendency to see them as in competition with each other to provide the best and most secure route to the truth. At worst this attitude can lead to intolerance and tensions in society, at best it leads to confusion. There appear to be two ways of establishing unity. One is to insist that my ideas and beliefs are the only true path to knowledge and so attempt to denigrate other paths by exposing them as defective, even heretical, either by verbal persuasion or, in extreme cases, physical violence. Another is to seek out what is valuable in the different approaches and using them to enrich one's understanding. In this book, Michael has chosen this latter way and it pays handsome dividends. Despite the superficial differences of the various wisdom traditions, there is much that unites their underlying messages. Chief of these is the concept of non-duality. But appreciation of the universality of this concept only takes one so far. We need to experience it in practice and this book helps with this aspect too by identifying how we can let this spirit of unity permeate our day-to-day lives.

John DeVal

Leader, School of Philosophy, Cambridge

INTRODUCTION

Imagine that you are at a party. The party banter wafts and washes around you, and the conversation ebbs and flows. Then someone mentions the subject of religion. At this stage, there is more often than not a "turn off" of attention—some folk try to move on, whilst others feel a bit trapped, like rabbits in the headlights of a car. But nonetheless, the conversation rolls on, perhaps rather on the following lines:

He: "Do you ever go to church?"

She: "Not if I can help it! Oh—maybe at Christmas."

He: "Or maybe the odd wedding or funeral."

She: "Yes, I suppose so. Otherwise, it all seems so ... well ..."

He: "Predictable. And, frankly, not particularly inspiring. They're always such nice folk at church but ... can't really put my finger on it."

She: "Well, I don't believe in God anyway, so there's not a lot of point."

He: "I dunno. What I can't get my head around is if the Christian God is the real deal, the only OK one, and the Islamists say the same, so do the Jews and everyone else, they can't all be right, can they?"

She: "Er, no. As I said, can't see the point of religion."

He: "Hmm. I can't either if I'm honest. But ... I still think there's *something*—don't know what to call it, but I do feel different if I'm, say, looking at a beautiful sunset, or admiring a fabulous view, or maybe entering a great cathedral. Not so much religious as ... but I suppose you could call it spiritual?"

She: "Well if you put it like that I suppose so. I must admit there are times when I feel a kind of ... not sure how to put this ... a oneness with nature, and when in that state I confess I do feel a bit better disposed to people around me than I do normally."

He: "What do you mean?"

She: "I suppose I'm not so separate—there's a kind of unity if you like. I can see how you could call that feeling spiritual in a funny kind of way. I don't see how that fits in with religion though."

He: "Nor do I. But it does make you wonder though, doesn't it?"

If any of that conversation resonates with you, then it is possible this book might work for you. My intention in writing it is not to try to prove anything, or to convince anyone of the rectitude of any particular path or belief system. The hope is that with the heart and mind open that questions will arise in the mind of the reader—questions of the type implied in the party conversation just read.

The book invites the reader to see if it is possible to discern a common thread, or unity, across and throughout all human beings in terms of their basic composition, and the wisdom traditions or civilisations that are evolved. This is despite today's uncertain and fear—driven world. We live in a fractious, disjointed, dysfunctional and seemingly entrenched materialist world today. No matter how much improved is our technological know—how, our information based methodology, or our results—driven culture, we seem to be behaving more and more like hamsters running on a wheel in a cage—running ever faster and faster, getting nowhere, and caged and bound. So the thinking was to provide something of an antidote, not by way of a quick fix, nor as a glib or facile endeavour to force something because it sounds as if it ought to be like that. No, it's more about discarding from our philosophical or mental wardrobe the musty clothes of the ephemeral, the habit—driven, the pretentious and the superficial.

If we do that, what then? Well—nothing! At least initially. I do not believe one needs immediately to don another set of philosophical clothing and risk returning to base. No, the recommendation is just to take a step back and look. Watch. Notice, when the mind is quiet, how you feel. Just observe. Let the senses play as they will, but without interference from the mind. And in the noticing and the observation maybe there will be a quiet depth of awareness, well removed from the flotsam and jetsam of everyday living and the life stuff that formerly seemed so all-consuming.

I would wish that whatever the belief system, creed, cultural, religious or educational background of the reader, that this book will encourage a genuine and heartfelt enquiry into what, really and truly, makes us humans human. If there is a depth, or awareness behind the obvious and the "life stuff" then what is it? Is it important and can it be accessed at will? Does it have any significance? What are the implications? What have the great teachers—the Socrates's, Jesus's, Buddha's of the world had to say about it? And how does modern science fit in, if at all?

The title of the book implies the need to investigate two things—philosophy and mindfulness. I am suggesting that by doing so we can enter a wholly different, deeper and somehow more "real" world than that which seems to be the lot for most of us most of the time. In fact, I would go so far as to say that coming to a proper comprehension of the true composition of oneself, that it is actually impossible not to gain admittance to a peaceful, fulfilled and contented state of being. In that state one is ready willing and able to offer service to one's fellow beings to a degree quite unimaginable to that available in "routine" mode, thus generating joy, unity and manifesting love ("Love makes the world go round—literally!")

The approach of what I am calling "mindful philosophy" is basically very practical and grounded. There is no need to have practiced either mindfulness or philosophy before. Academic prowess is not required (but don't eschew your critical faculties.). The idea is to see if there can be a rapprochement of the two notions, often seen as opposites rather than complimentary, of "faith" (or belief) and "reason" (discrimination, evaluation). It is my firm belief that this is indeed so. I believe that the book demonstrates that right across the footprint of human history for thousands of years right up to and including the present day, inclusive of the data from modern science and many of our greatest twenty-first century writers and thinkers, can be discerned a golden thread. This is the golden thread of spirituality, of essence, of *unity*, which transcends all the specific wisdom traditions, but lies immanent in all of them.

This book falls into three sections—the what, where, and how of mindful philosophy. The "what" comprises the first two chapters, setting the scene and defining our terms of reference. The bulk of the book is contained within the "where", so that we take relatively brief looks at many of the great wisdom traditions in the world, both past and present, to see how we might discern this golden thread of non-duality or unity, how it manifests, how it might be recognised and where it has been/is being appreciated. Finally, the "how" is intended to provide some ideas, practices and guidance as to how to take this forward; how the golden thread might be woven into a fine and gorgeous garment, fit for all of us to wear.

Finally, I should make it clear that all the views, opinions and analysis in this book are entirely my own, and are not purported to belong to, or be representative of, any group, religion, school or other organisation of any sort.

PART 1

MINDFUL PHILOSOPHY: THE WHY

CHAPTER 1

AN INTRODUCTION TO MINDFUL PHILOSOPHY

The purpose of life is to find out who and what you really are. Those picking up a book like this will probably already be seeking deeply, looking at themselves and their life situations and asking some searching questions, such as the following:

- How are true peace and contentment found? Can they be found at all?
- What is a human being?
- Who *really* am I?
- Am I this entity called Joe Bloggs, who is six feet tall, who is married to Mary Bloggs, who runs a home, and who has a mortgage, a couple of kids, and a particular self-image? Or is there something more?
- What's the point of it all? Is there any meaning to my life?

Well, this book does not purport to give the answers. But it might, if carefully read and used, assist the human life traveller to find direction in

1

self-discovery by rearranging the list of priorities of what really is important and what is ephemeral. And in so doing, I can at least promise one thing: life will open to that which brings joy and uplift, peace and contentment, and steadiness of being.

We are going to take something of a rollercoaster ride in our quest for self-discovery. In our peregrinations, we first will be considering what this idea of "mindful philosophy" is and why it might be important in the twenty-first century, when there appears to be a spiritual reappraisal taking place. The apparent demise or lack of trust and acceptance of established religions in many quarters seems to be replaced by a plethora of seedlings of non-establishment spirituality.

It must be said at once that the apparent loss of influence in many of the mainstream religions doesn't negate their validity. Indeed, one of the things shown up by mindful philosophy is the amount of common ground that exists across the great wisdom traditions of the world. The fact that this can be so difficult to appreciate is because far too rarely our approach to such issues is carried out *mindfully.* It is one thing to put the truth first, but quite another to place my view of the truth—suitably elaborated with belief systems, codes of conduct, religious and political standpoints, and the rest—at the head of the priority list.

So we will look at what unites us. It is so easy to dwell upon the things that divide us. A few moments looking at the news will soon convince us of that. This process is called *non-duality*. It's the connecting thread that runs through this book. The essence of this teaching is to make real the essential unity of all of us: east and west, male and female, black and white, young and old, and so on. This is a process of *discovery,* or *"dis – covery"*. It's taking away the covering that seems to enshroud the being.

We will take a fresh look at where and how non-dual or mindful teaching can be found underpinning most, if not all, of the great wisdom and religious teachings—even if this is neither recognised nor espoused by the most enthusiastic proponents of these traditions. In the West, these teachings could be called the "perennial philosophy,"[1] with roots in ancient Egypt and flowering in a variety of habitats thereafter, including the true essence of much of Christian teaching, notably the Gnostics. We visit Socrates and Plato and the Neoplatonists and the Italian Renaissance, courtesy of one Marsilio Ficino. There are several later figures, including Emerson in the nineteenth-century United States. We will consider the indigenous traditions from Africa, Australia, the United States, and elsewhere. We are going to see whether the luminaries of today, such as Eckhart Tolle, Deepak Chopra, and Ken Wilber, can help us. And finally, we will consider whether modern science can help us comprehend spirituality by using the most up-to-date research.

From the East, we have the Advaita Vedanta tradition from India, Sufiism, and certain of the Buddhist pathways, such as Mahayana Buddhism. And non-duality can be seen in the Ubuntu tradition emanating from parts of Africa and the Native American tradition as well as within the Celtic tradition of Ireland and the Western Isles.

I suggest that in all the great spiritual traditions of the world, either overtly or covertly, lies a single great truth—that there is only one ultimate non-dual reality and that the true essence or the real *self* of human beings is not separate from that reality. We will consider the implications of this later, but for the moment, one can reflect upon the fact that this truth is available to all people at all times. And we will consider, from a very practical and feet-on-the-ground perspective, what this all means for you and me, here and now.

There is a term—*self-realisation*—used to describe this process. This means the true essence of the human being can actually be made real. This process can be helped along by using the great wisdom traditions of the world as outlined above, but some care is needed; without guidance, the many distortions that accumulate over time as humankind interprets then reinterprets the great scriptural guidance from across the globe can lead to confusion and blind alleys. This is where the twin disciplines of mindfulness and philosophy come in. The former gives us clarity as to the methodology regarding how we implement the advice given, and the latter provides the necessary advice and guidance bereft of considerations of power and influence, financial pressures, and most importantly, any ego-based motivation of whatever sort.

To clarify these issues, we will now take a closer look at these two notions of mindfulness and philosophy.

Philosophy

On the face of it, the two notions of philosophy and mindfulness have little to unite them. Typically, the philosopher is perceived as lost in the world of academe, consumed by the need to analyse, all head and not a lot of heart, and maybe all a bit dry. Well, this is not so. The opposite is probably nearer the mark. And mindfulness is often simply perceived as just a therapeutic process with Buddhist overtones. Again, not so.

Let me explain.

The literal meaning of the word *philosophy* is "love of wisdom." It is derived from a pair of Greek words: *philo,* meaning "love of," and *sophia,* meaning "wisdom." So the philosopher is the lover of wisdom. I'm going to suggest that you, the reader, are a philosopher. After all, why did you pick up and start to read this book? Surely your desire to find out about the world and your place in it means that at some level you love wisdom.

What matters more than anything else to the philosopher is the truth. Not a belief system, not a view, not a preferred take on life, but that which is truthful. How we get to that stage is a different matter, of course, and I will address it below.

Wisdom then is the goal. It may be defined as "whatever knowledge, teaching, or advice that enables life to be led in a more truthful, contented, and happy manner."

If I ask, "Are you wise?" I can understand that you would probably offer a negative response, such being the natural diffidence of most people. However, I suggest that if I were to ask you to get a pen and paper and then jot down the words that best describe someone you would consider wise, I'm sure you would have no difficulty in making quite a long list. How about these as a start?

- magnanimous and tolerant
- reasonable
- perceptive
- well disposed
- loving and caring
- steady and steadfast
- non-judgemental
- attentive and present

You will probably be able to add quite a lot more. Now if this is so, and you recognise this to be so, does this not imply that some of this knowledge already resides in you? Otherwise, how would you recognise it as valid evidence of wisdom? Is there not some resonance within that is activated by simply applying one's attention to the concept of wisdom? And what does this tell us about ourselves?

Certainly, one does not need to gain qualifications to obtain such qualities, which are manifest right across the spectrum of humanity, whether educated or not. This, in turn, indicates that there is a world of difference between wisdom, as defined above, and information. One can possess qualifications, university degrees, and technical knowledge of all types, but that in itself doesn't make us wise people, does it? I certainly don't decry good and appropriate learning, but it is clear that something else is needed. And, yes, that can be taught up to a point, but what is more important is to keep appropriate company, to endeavour to put into place in a practical manner the words of the wise, and to observe what happens. This process could be described as gaining true knowledge because it is based on dispassionate, objective observation that is not coloured by any stance or perspective. This boils down to truth.

The motivation of the true philosopher is to discover and realise the truth, devoid of any other considerations of any sort. This is a very high ideal, and explains why for some the study of philosophy and implementing its practices is the highest goal for the human being to pursue. And the good news is that this is the birthright of every human being and not just the academically gifted, the intellectually driven, or those motivated by considerations of prowess, success, or prestige.

This type of approach helps us to keep grounded. It is highly practical. Whilst there is no need to eschew the world of books and dissertations, the mindful or non-dual philosopher is basically operating in the ordinary world of family, work, relationships, and all the day-to-day stuff of life. And in so doing, she or he can indeed start to have a take on the great issues and questions which are the stuff of philosophy—the questions I posed right at the start of this chapter, for example.

This is because the wise, or the mindful philosopher, can control and so make best use of that most valuable tool in the kit bag—the mind. There is a perception of what is appropriate *now*. There is knowledge as to how the meeting of the need of the moment should be approached. This is because to apply philosophical principles in this manner enables a sense of proportion to be availed. And this is where there seems to be a real interface with mindfulness.

Mindfulness

Mindfulness has become something of a buzzword today. Indeed, one of the wonders of the era in which we live is the fact that mindfulness has brought a degree of peace and tranquillity to many thousands of people, many of whom are not "religious" in any shape or form, and would possibly not describe themselves as particularly "spiritual" either. Mindfulness classes are springing up in village halls throughout the land, in places of work, and, I understand, even in the seat of government.

The word *mindful* means "aware". Mindfulness is awareness. If one is mindful of something, be it the neighbour's dog or the presence of a great being, one is simply aware of that presence. The current popularity of mindfulness is in no small measure due to the teachings of the American writer and mindfulness teacher, Jon Kabat-Zinn. Formerly a Jewish microbiologist, he investigated the extent to which chronic pain could be assisted by meditative training. He was able to research the subject, and with a number of cognitive behaviour therapists achieved a marked degree of success in these fields. These and others were successful in capturing and harnessing international media attention on the subject of mindfulness, ultimately successfully establishing the mindfulness-based cognitive therapy (MBCT) and stress-reduction (MBSR) programs.

Kabat-Zinn has defined mindfulness as "paying attention, in a particular way, on purpose, in the present moment, non-judgementally".[2] He had studied under the well-known Buddhist master Thich Nhat Hanh, who has written widely around the subject. Now this definition is very succinct, and provides an insight which covers both that which is explicit about mindfulness, as well as what is implicit. We will be looking in more detail at this later, but for now it's worth reflecting that *attention* is a key concept because without it there is nothing. The *present moment* likewise—the only thing one really has is *now*. And to operate *non-judgementally* is essential if we are to consider anything as it really is, and not be tainted with a film of particular, personal views, opinions, or belief systems.

Mindfulness is consistently referred to by the Buddha in his teachings, within which it appears as part of a system known as the *noble eightfold path*. This outlines eight essential facets, designed to help the human being to evolve in the three areas of moral conduct, mental discipline, and wisdom. So one can see immediately that there is a significant philosophical involvement in this teaching. Mindfulness is the seventh item. All need to be practiced simultaneously. Mindfulness, or "right mindfulness", is said to comprise being fully aware of all facets of human activity, including the body and its functions, the world of emotions and feelings, the activities of the mind and mental activity, such as thoughts, ideas, and conceptions.

Mindfulness is not exclusively Buddhist. In fact, this teaching is clearly availed in the Advaita or non-dual teaching from India, sometimes referred to as the mystical side of Hinduism. The twentieth century teacher Nisargadatta Maharaj has already been referred to in the opening pages at the start of this book, in his reference to dealing with a question on how to deal with negative emotions through allowing the mind to quieten, where he states that *All that matters is mindfulness, total awareness of oneself, or rather of ones mind.* It can also be discerned in the deeper Christian teachings, too. The Orthodox tradition has a meditative process referred to as *watchfulness*. Much of the appeal of mindfulness lies in the fact that by its very nature it transcends boundaries, whether religious, cultural, or traditional. So again, we see that we are inevitably drawn into considerations of non-duality, which is a notion we will consider in depth in the next chapter.

The most well-known areas where mindfulness is encountered today are within the world of therapy as practiced by Kabat-Zinn. There are many books on the subject, and courses such as the most useful eight-week programme offered by Mark Williams and Danny Penman both in their book offering *Mindfulness: A Practical Guide to Finding Peace in a Frantic World* and the helpful CD attached to it.[3] This is an excellent way to commence a study of mindfulness in this tradition and, as a succinct introduction to this subject, is something I would heartily recommend. However, I think a word of caution is necessary.

Mindfulness was not promulgated by its Buddhist and other originators as primarily a therapeutic tool, no matter how efficacious it may be in that direction. It forms part of a spiritual path. To fully comprehend the true essence and direction of travel of mindfulness teaching, something more is needed. The non-dual philosopher therefore needs to look behind and beyond the world of therapy. Without in any way wishing to detract from this most valuable area, if one refers back to Thich Nhat Hanh, we find a rather different approach, which fully embraces the notion of spirituality, which is not something courted by what one might call "therapeutic mindfulness".

Here is a quote from his book *Going Home*.[4] He takes a mundane human activity such as eating a piece of bread. He says,

> *When we hold a piece of bread to eat, if mindfulness is there, if the Holy Spirit is there, we can eat the bread in a way that will allow us to touch the whole cosmos deeply. A piece of bread contains the sunshine. That is not something difficult to see. Without sunshine, the piece of bread cannot be. A piece of bread contains a cloud. Without a cloud, the wheat cannot grow. So, when you eat a piece of bread, you eat the cloud, you eat the sunshine, you eat the minerals, time, space, everything. One thing contains everything. With the energy of mindfulness, we can see deeply. With the Holy Spirit, we can see deeply. Mindfulness is the energy of the Buddha. The Holy Spirit is the energy of God. They have the capacity to make us present, deeply understanding, and loving.*

He continues to outline that if we do not live each moment deeply, there is no way we can touch the ultimate dimension, the dimension of the noumenon (that which exists but is devoid of perception or sense, to be contrasted with phenomenon).

So we have moved away from therapy to the placing of mindfulness in a spiritual and philosophical context. If mindfulness has to do with energy in spiritual terms (Holy Spirit, Buddha), then it is placed firmly and squarely within the realm of non-dual philosophy. Non-dual, because as I will demonstrate in chapter 2, it does not acknowledge the supremacy of any particular creed or tradition, but simply the conscious awareness that is common to all human beings irrespective of race, religion, tradition, place, custom, or education.

Mindful philosophy is therefore a synthesis between the two complementary disciplines of mindfulness and philosophy. It appraises the common ground between awareness and wisdom and the love thereof. It involves consideration of all aspects of what the human being is comprised, including and in particular, the spiritual dimension. There is a very practical aspect to all of this, because quite clearly no matter how high minded our theories of human spirituality might be, if they cannot be put to work within the coal face of life by "Mr and Mrs Everyman", then they are not a lot of use. And this in turn involves guidance as to how and from whom the mindful philosophy teachings might be availed.

These are big issues. They are very germane in the twenty-first century. Indeed, one has to ask can there be a more important or more relevant area for study and reflection than these fundamental human attributes? The fundamentals of what constitutes a human being and the potential for realisation in each and every one of us are universal. A full understanding of these principles reveals that ultimately there cannot be any separation between us. It is for these reasons that the pursuit of mindful philosophy could equally well be described as *non-dual philosophy*, which is a concept we will now investigate.

CHAPTER 2

NON-DUAL PHILOSOPHY

Non-duality is basically a perception. It's an understanding, and it is something to be derived from personal experience of life rather than simply by philosophical discourse. If there are many great teachers who directly espouse, or indirectly imply, that essentially "all is one", and that there are in truth no boundaries between us, then this is more a matter of applying this as a principle of living than an academic concept. We can apply principles of non-duality in each and every walk of life. It's a case of attitude or the intention behind the action. Here is a brief tale outlining how this takes place:

> There was once upon a time a wise man, leaning on a gate in contemplation of the prospect in front of him. On his left lay a pathway which ultimately led to a village in the valley below. On his right the same pathway led up the hill to another village.
>
> It so happened that a traveller came from the lower village and, looking somewhat tight faced and out of sorts, said as he passed the

wise man, "Well. What a rotten lot. I wouldn't go down to that village if I were you. They are so miserable."

"Guess you'll find them like that up there as well." said the wise man, indicating the upper village. The traveller went his way.

Next day, the same wise man was leaning on the same gate. And another traveller appeared from the lower village. This time he was of bonny complexion, bright, and cheery, and he said to the wise man, "They're a great crowd down there—everyone is so bright and helpful. Didn't want to go away."

"Guess you'll find them like that up there as well." said the wise man. The traveller went his way.

Now the wise man was seen to be wise because his attention was on every facet of the scenario. He was able to read the situation to the extent that, just by looking and listening to the sounds of the voices of the two travellers, he was able to comprehend how they would fare in the upper village. Notice that he didn't judge the situation—he simply told it as it was. The story illustrates that the attitude we take governs how we're perceived in society and how we're reacted to. It's our choice. We need to exercise that choice. And we can do that by investing a greater or lesser level of consciousness, or "nous", into the situation. This can be either from the perspective of unity, inclusivity, and understanding (second traveller) or from division, exclusivity, and ignorance (first traveller).

Four Precepts for Non-Dual Philosophy

To gain some knowledge of the direction of travel of mindful philosophy, there are four precepts which permeate wherever this guidance can be found, and which illustrate where we're coming from. They are

- There is a Supreme Being, or the Absolute. This is real. Everything else is transient.

- The true self of humankind is not separate from and is identical in essence to the Supreme Being, or Absolute.

- The purpose of life is to come to the realisation that this is so. This realisation can take place via the normal duties of life.

- This realisation will produce unlimited bliss, happiness, contentment, and steadiness of being, and the capacity to assist others in this direction.

These precepts, or similar versions thereof, can be discerned running throughout the wisdom traditions of the world. Another version is outlined in chapter 8, emanating from the teaching of Aldous Huxley in his book on *The Perennial Philosophy*. The version I have used here has been adapted from the definition used by a London—based non-dual organisation predominantly espousing the Indian tradition of Advaita Vedanta, known as Shanti Sadan, together with material produced by the School of Economic Science, also London-based but worldwide in terms of various philosophy schools teaching practical philosophy on a non-dual basis.[1]

We will now take a closer look at the implications of these precepts:

1) The Supreme Being is real, and all else is transient.

The precept states that the Absolute, or Supreme Being, is the ultimate reality. It is probably impossible to define what this means. The Absolute cannot be quantified or appraised in any way. It is not availed via sensory perception. In such circumstances, one needs to take refuge in the words of the wise or from writings of the highest calibre. In chapter 2 of the Indian spiritual classic, the Bhagavad Gita, this Self (capital "S") of man, or spiritual essence, is described as being indestructible, immortal, unborn, always the same. (as opposed to the "self" – the persona – please see on for explanation).

The Bhagavad Gita continues, "Weapons cleave it not, fire burns it not, water drenches it not, and wind dries it not. It is impenetrable; it can neither be drowned or scorched, nor dried. It is Eternal, all—pervading, Unchanging, Immovable and Most Ancient." Whatever it might be is impossible to substantiate, so in that tradition the words from the Brihadaranyaka Upanishad—"But the spirit is not this, is not this"—are the closest one can get to comprehending this ultimate reality.

So, where does this leave God? And does the mindful philosopher believe in God? Well, it depends entirely upon what is being discussed. The notion of a supreme being does sound rather biblical, and looked at from the viewpoint of non-duality, the idea of an elderly gentleman perched somewhat precariously upon a cloud as delineated in the ceiling of the Sistine Chapel would be unlikely to find favour. Such an individual deity is said to be most upset if his will is not undertaken, and indeed can upon occasion become jealous. But jealous of what? That implies another even more supreme being, does it not?

Under non-dual teachings, this seems somewhat preposterous. But that does not negate the notion of an ultimate non-dual reality or absolute essence. We can refer to this as God, amongst other nomenclature. Now let us suppose I believe in God or a supreme being and that you don't. I cannot prove to you the existence of this supreme being. And you cannot prove to me that there is no such thing. We might well argue around this long and hard for hours and indeed days. So we have an impasse, do we not? But I am going to suggest to you that it is perfectly possible for you to prove to *yourself* the existence of such a being, should you wish to do so. That is where techniques such as meditation and contemplation bear fruit—anything that allows the mind to quieten, so that we can just *be*.

Under the guidance of non-duality, the idea of a supreme being has to be depersonalised so that it becomes not a question of me here and my god somewhere over there. It is only by integrating or merging with the supreme being that there can ever be any comprehension of what is meant by the term. In other words, one has to cease identifying with all that one is not. The famous British philosopher Paul Brunton in his book *The Inner Reality* relates a discussion with the materialist French astronomer Lalonde when the latter remarked, "I have swept the heavens with my telescope but have not come across a God." Brunton's response was to state, "Alas, he had but to put his telescope aside, still his mind, and there God would be found."[2]

And therein lies the clue, and sets a direction of travel for the mindful philosopher. I will be appraising this later, but for the moment, maybe we can see that underpinning and supporting all that seems to comprise this creation is this undefinable essence. This becomes more apparent to those who meditate, or have the ability to fall completely still, so that the mind is dormant and one is just left with being, awareness, consciousness—call it what you will.

2) **The self of humankind in essence is identical to the Supreme Being, or Absolute.**

This is the great truth which underpins the wisdom traditions across the globe. So it is of concern that to some fundamentalist adherents to these traditions (notably the monotheist traditions of Middle Eastern origin) that such a statement is perceived as blasphemous. Nothing could be further from the truth. But this is not something that can be taught or instructed. It is a matter of personal experience. There is no reason why, particularly if one has recourse to good company or a sympathetic guide, or both, anyone cannot apprehend this.

Paul Brunton's remark is germane here. For it is down to us—to our real Selves—to emerge like butterflies coming away from their chrysalises—to discover this personally. (Note the word *discover*. It means literally removing and discarding that which covers our true Selves, or our true lights.) This is what was meant by the words inscribed over the oracle at Delphi: "Man, know thySelf." And it is what Shakespeare is referring to in Hamlet where these words appear: "This above all: to thine own Self be true, and it must follow, as the night the day, thou canst not then be false to any man." This appears also in the Christian tradition where under both St Matthew's and St Mark's gospels, the second great commandment is to "love your neighbour as yourself". This could equally have been stated as the Self. (Capital "S" in Self my alteration.)

How can this self be in any way separated from the Divine? This precept spells out that ultimately humans are not animals functioning solely on the gross or sensory level. Nor are we mechanistic automatons ruled only by the world of mind, with all of its tendencies and proclivities— likes/dislikes, opinions, belief systems, habits, desires/aversions, fears and prejudices, and ego-driven concerns. Humans are Divine beings before they are anything else. And that is something with which every one of us can engage and manifest in terms of how we live our lives and what values we seek to implement.

3) The purpose of life is to discover that this is so. This can be carried out within the normal duties of life.

It is not necessary to lock oneself away in a monastery or seminary. It is not necessary either to go miles away or to do anything outside normal living. Nor does one need to go off to academe and get qualified in philosophy, religion, logic, or other discipline. The fact is that we are that which we seek. It's a little like the tale of the very thirsty fish from the Sikh teacher Kabir: "I laugh when I hear that the fish in the water is thirsty. Can you not see how the Absolute is in your own house, as you wander from forest to forest so listlessly? In your home is the Truth. Go where you want; to Benares or to Mathura; if your soul is a stranger to you then then so is the whole world."

What is necessary is that we simply use the gifts we have, listen to the words of the wise, and put them into practice. This is where the practices of what is now referred to as *mindfulness* are required. By using the power of attention—either focussed or open—and by being fully present here and now, the truth of what we are may be availed. This process involves what Plato called "right use of the mind", which is another thread running right through the various non-dual traditions. It forms the subject of the book by the English nineteenth-century philosopher James Allen called *As a Man Thinketh*, which succinctly and most clearly puts this point across.

And in the output from the twenty-first century one finds this being referred to again and again, whether via Eckhart Tolle in his wonderful book on presence called *The Power of Now*, Ken Wilber in his integrationalist teaching, or the many holistic therapeutic organisations covering psychotherapy, psychosynthesis, Gestalt, and many others.

We will be taking a closer look at this general area in chapter 8. For the moment, perhaps this illustrates why this pathway can be described as *mindful* philosophy. And we need to hear the words of the wise not as we think they ought to be, but as they are. So we need to eschew the ubiquitous tendency to judge, and instead, through a calm, still, and steady state to simply live life. We need, literally, to come to our senses—seeing, touching, scenting, tasting, and most importantly, listening.

In chapter 1, we considered what constitutes a wise person. To take this a stage further, one needs to make endeavours to find out what exactly is meant by wisdom or by the idea of knowledge which takes us forward in the direction of truth and well-being. And what really do we mean by the notion that "all is one"? These important issues will be considered later, but for the moment, perhaps we can accept that in virtually all open minded and well-disposed people there does occur from time to time deep and heartfelt questions, such as "What is the point of it all?" "Where and how should I live?" and the deepest of them all, "Who and what, in truth, am I?"

In non-dual philosophy to perceive and to merge with the essential unity or oneness is the goal. To be united is tantamount to being content. Human beings are at their happiest when they feel bonded, together, integrated, and meaningful. They are at their most miserable when they are separate, isolated, excluded, and meaningless. Now why should this be? The answer is that the former is a natural state, whereas the latter is not. The former is an example of what results when the ego or persona clears off out of the way. The latter exemplifies what takes place when ego concerns such as fear—driven desires, ideas, aversions, and the like are allowed to run riot.

Big I/ Little I

To explain further, in non-dual philosophy (amongst others), there is the notion of "big I" and "little I". Big I is your natural unlimited unconditioned Self, described under precept two above, whose function is simply to be. This does not mean an existence of negativity. It means full engagement with whatever confronts one, but in a manner that is detached; not worried about the end result; devoid of ideas of image, status, role, and position in society. So one meets whatever need creation throws up without criticism, in a state of calm serenity, and so one can turn the other cheek, if that is what is required, without rancour and without any claim on the outcome.

Little I, by contrast, is hugely concerned about all of the above. Little I is not what "I am" but what I think I am. The main concern underpinning little I is fear—fear of annihilation, and worried that life is throwing up problems both actual and (in particular) potential that will deprive it of happiness and well-being. This is not a problem of concern to big I, who relies instead upon his or her true nature to deal with life's issues and conundrums.

The big I/little I model is found in a number of teachings and walks of life. The renowned Swiss psychologist Carl Jung saw it as the real Self as opposed to what he termed the *persona*. And similarly, the Gestalt therapy teaching is to consider the matter by way of little I being an image of the real Self, but not the Self as such.

The Vedic tradition, from which we have the Advaita (a Sanskrit term meaning literally "not two") refers to *Aham*, meaning, "I am" (note how close in sound the Sanskrit is to the English). This is contrasted with *ahankara*, which means "ego," but is derived from the addition to

Aham of something, anything. It can be seen as the vehicle for Aham, or an addition, and so a limitation placed over Aham/self.

So if we identify with a role such as a job description, or a gender, stereotype, image, idea of oneself, or whatever, at the expense of simply being "I", or the self, then we have moved away from unity to multiplicity, from the universal to the individual, or from self to ego/persona. There is, of course, nothing inherently wrong with any of these roles/beliefs. It is simply that they are best used as a means of meeting the need at the time—not as a rigid identification covering our essential being.

If we are mindful, or aware, then we will not fall into this trap because we will have enough presence about us to recognise warning signs—like feelings of fear about possible threats to our status (someone else is doing it better maybe.), or worries about some issue like getting there on time, how one will deal with a forthcoming meeting, what the boss might say, and so on. It is much better to keep steady with big I and stay in the present moment than it is to indulge the fears and fantasies of little I, which occupies any ground other than the present moment as its fears/fantasies are all dealing with hypothetical concerns which might or might not happen in the future, or reliving experiences and happenings in the past.

4) **The result of this realisation is unlimited contentment, well-being, steadiness of being, and the capacity to assist others along the way.**

So there we have it. It seems so easy, put like that, but for most of us to end up in that state is likely to require some fundamental reappraisals of how we are conducting our affairs. But if one thinks for one moment and invites the question *what would life be like if there were no desires?* one might just get a feel for what is on offer. If you are without desire, you are content. If you are content, you are happy. If you are happy, then that is a supreme state, if it's genuine. True happiness is not pleasure, derived from some object of the senses, and almost inevitably followed by pain as the source of the "happiness" is removed.

Nor is it "happiness" due to the achievement of some goal, the ticking of some box of life, for removal or undermining of such a goal will probably mean the opposite of happiness—misery—experienced in short order. No, the realisation of the unity of the self with the Divine produces well-being of a wholly different order—happiness not dependent upon some *thing* but self-dependent. To this, there is no down side. There is no opposite. And as will be outlined below, this is the inalienable right for all humans to experience if the priorities of life are arranged in line with these precepts.

To be free of desires means living in a steady and secure state. If one reflects for one moment, it will become apparent that one is truly and completely content when there are no desires in the mind for things to be other than as they are. In that state, one is in the best possible condition to see where help can be brought to assist and care for other fellow travellers along the highways and byways of life. Put another way, the natural love and compassion which we all can recognise is fully and uninhibitedly availed. One does not do this out of ego-fuelled desires or ambition. Rather, it is born of a simple and humble attitude to meet the need of the situation, not the need of my desires, my likes, my ambitions, and so on.

The Threefold Nature of the Self (Big I)

Non-duality, by its very nature, seeks that which unites, and identifies where there is common ground. One of the most important areas where this is evident is via three areas common to every human being which comprise our essential natures. They are truth, consciousness (or true being), and bliss (or true contentment and happiness). In fact, these three are simply three aspects of the same thing, but they are usually approached individually and referred to as such in the ancient Vedic language of Sanskrit, where they are known as *satchitananda*. This is a composite word, comprised of the three words: *sat, chit,* and *ananda. Sat* means "truth" (the English word *satisfaction* is a derivative), *chit* means "consciousness", and *ananda* means "bliss".

Now so far as *sat*, or truth, is concerned, no one would knowingly seek untruth. Truth is utterly fundamental, even down to the extent that the bank robber with his bag of swag seeks the truth as to the exit from the bank—not the untruth. Truth is not about my truth and your truth, valid though these views might be. Truth is about intention. It's where one is coming from. not where one is going to. The problem with *true for me/you* is that that is essentially a belief system evolved from one's life experiences. There is, of course, nothing wrong with that, but the view must of necessity be partial and open to review in the event of new/different life experiences. It is "qualified truth", not real truth.

Truth is that which is permanent. It has a sound when uttered, this being of quiet authority and gentle but massive power. We talk about "the ring of truth", do we not? And this recognition and need is common to every human being. Any parent will recognise by way of the sound in the voice when the child is speaking truthfully or when he or she is trying to pull the wool over the parent's eyes.

The second facet is that of consciousness, or being. It's natural to value life at all costs. There is nothing more important. And it implies a depth of being, true existence, or "is-ness". The direction is away from doing and towards being. This is a huge area, but it underpins all that we experience. It's the blank canvas of being upon which we paint our picture of doing. And there's no human being to which this does not apply.

Lastly, happiness, or bliss, is the goal of every decision we take. This is because no human being would knowingly court misery. We all want to be happy—all the time. Whilst we might have strong views as to how this might be achieved, the fact is that we arrange our decision-making processes by selecting the choice that we think will create the most happiness. And, yes, this happiness or well-being can be for me, or it can be for a wider concern (family, group, nation, universe), but ultimately one cannot avoid complying with the universal and wholly natural tendency to maximise happiness and well-being. Indeed, there are various references to what's known as the "cosmic joke". The great teachers, having realised that they are not the small, limited selves we have called "little I", but are the immortal, imperishable selves not separate from either the Absolute or from all other beings, find this laughable. This goes back to the "thirsty fish"—they have realised that after a lifetimes search they *are* what they *seek*, and were always so, and there never was anywhere to go, anything to achieve, or anything to do after all. So we hear tales of the laughing Buddha, the joyful Christ, or the playful Krishna.

There are sundry tales around this point. In the Sufi tradition there is the following:

> *There was once a man who lived in a house in Baghdad. He had a vivid dream that in Cairo that there was great treasure in a particular house there. So he gathered himself, and set off through the desert, and made his way eventually to Cairo. In the process he experienced many difficulties on his journey, but eventually he found his way to the address given. Upon arrival at the house he met the owner. The owner explained that funnily enough he also had had a dream, this time identifying the existence of treasure at a house in Baghdad—which the traveller recognised as his own house. So back went the traveller, and sure enough there was the treasure.*

This story explains that we are what we seek. The treasure is the knowledge that one is the self—big I, and not the ego entity or persona—little I. The journey through the desert is the life story, with all its ups and downs. The irony is that it's necessary to go through all the vicissitudes of life to realise—make real—what we had all the time. This is sometimes heard as "the pathless path" or the "gateless gate", in both the Zen and Sufi non-dual teachings. The path is again the life story, sometimes encountering great obstacles or even personal tragedy, illness, or loss which makes one completely reappraise where one is and so facing up to the need to make major adjustments. These might be by turning away from selfish and indulgent behaviour, from dogmatic beliefs, or from materialist limiting perceptions. These often create disillusionment, despair, and hopelessness—such things sadly can be the only apparent way to make us turn to the reality of who we really are and what life is about. As says the Sufi sage and poet Rumi: "The pathless path opens whenever you genuinely say: 'There is no reality but the Absolute. There is only the Absolute.'"[3]

In a similar vein is the tale of three men who had spent their whole lives trying to scale a wall. Ultimately, they made it and burst out laughing. The first man fell down the wall on the far side, and disappeared from view, laughing away. The second man fell back, not without certain personal injuries, but still laughing. And the third man, laughing, came back to help his friends and companions. And why were they laughing? Because there was no wall. There never was a wall in the first place.

So, the nature of yourself and myself is truth, consciousness, and bliss. These are very deep, and transcend ego concerns such as pleasure/pain, good/bad, black/white, and the many pairs of opposites, not to mention all the multifarious bits and pieces of life, referred to in the Taoist tradition as "the 10,000 things".

Put another way, truth can be said to equate with being. Consciousness can be likened to the quiet, deep acknowledgement of that being. And true bliss is what quite simply and naturally arises as a result of that acknowledgement, or knowledge. And that is your and my nature. It's also the birthright of every human being to discover that to be so. As is said in the vernacular, what's not to like?

All Is One?

This is an oft-quoted phrase which at times tends to be offered almost as an excuse rather than as a serious philosophical statement. But it's demonstrably true if we implement the teachings of non-duality. Thus far, we have considered advice from the great world traditions of wisdom, but that doesn't mean to say that there aren't many and various teachers espousing non-duality today who aren't particularly concerned to be aligned with any particular tradition, but who seek to reveal by their teachings the fundamental common ground of all by using criteria which I believe comply with the general thrust of the four precepts above.

Amongst many options, I can recommend Eckhart Tolle's masterpieces *The Power of Now*, to which I have already made reference, and *A New Earth*; the many books of the Vietnamese master of mindfulness teaching, Thich Nhat Hanh; the integrationist methods of the American philosopher Ken Wilber; Tim Freke with his refreshingly candid and accessible approach on unity, using the notion of allowing both/and to replace the ego ideas of either/or. This is an important strand of non-dual thinking and has been featured in a number of authors, including the late New Zealand biologist/ philosopher Darryl Reanney.

There are many more, as outlined at the end of this chapter. If mindful philosophy is to resonate with seekers today, it needs to be made accessible in the language and usages of today. Fundamentally this philosophy needs to be seen not as a historic relic interesting primarily for the manner in which it illuminates past traditions (which, of course, it does), but as an experiential tool of living fit for the here and now in the twenty-first century. We are indeed fortunate to be living at a time when there seems to be a renaissance of spiritual teaching which is easily accessible, also easy to assimilate, and which does not have the requirement to sign up to anyone's particular creed or belief system.

To make this a little more credible, let's take a practical example. If "all is one", then it needs to be evident that there are no boundaries and that there is no separation between you and me and—well—everything and anything. Under the guidance of non-dual/mindful philosophy, there is nothing beyond the ultimate reality. This means that ultimately there is no such thing as a separate entity or separate being. There is, in truth, despite appearances, no such thing as a separate ego persona. This explains the ultimate fear of the ego or persona—which is its ultimate and inevitable annihilation. All this is transient, as stated in precept one.

So take a look at the page of this book which you are now reading. Ask yourself, what is this page? Is it the ultimate substratum of its genre, or is there something else about it that we can see? What, for example, if you tear it out, screw it up, and throw it. What is it then? A page? No. It is now a ball. It has changed from the form of page to the form of ball. But essentially, both forms, page and ball, are one thing—paper. In the first case, the form was rectilinear, two-dimensional and composite, part of a number of similar forms called *book*. In the latter case, the form was spherical, three dimensional, and multifaceted. Now these adjectives are simply attributes of the composite substance of paper.

So, if paper is now appearing real and substantial, we need to enquire, what is paper? The scientists will advise that paper is actually a composite form of cell nuclei which upon close examination will be found to comprise cellulose, carbon, hydrogen, and other chemical elements in various proportions. So have we now discovered what *page* is? It's all these chemicals arranged together as outlined by the physicist, is it not?

Well, no. Upon further and closer examination, we discover that all these chemicals comprise various DNA particles, chromosomes, and so on. So are these the final substantive article? No. Because each of these DNA strands, chromosomes and the like are formed of molecules, and these are formed of a particular banding of atoms. So—at last—is it the atom which is the ultimate essence of our page? No. Because the atoms are made up of minute particles called electrons, protons, and neutrons. They move about to such an extent that they are basically just energy.

This is what led Albert Einstein to evolve his famous theory of relativity, to the effect that the humble atom is not what it appears, because it is basically energy, and that matter as such does not exist. There seems to be simply the whizzing around of tiny particles of apparently solid matter. Is this, then, the ultimate substantive essence of our page? No. It seems that we now have one of the many paradoxes which permeate the study of mindful philosophy. An electron can be a wave and a particle at the same time. But if one applies consciousness to the wave in question, the wave becomes a particle.

So, in the last resort, the scientists are telling us that (i) there is no such thing as matter, and (ii) only by the application of attention, or consciousness can energy be reduced to become matter. This is material with which we will be engaging in chapter 9, where we will be considering how modern scientific research and methodology have, rather to the surprise of many research scientists, actually verified rather than negated the spiritual principles upon which mindful philosophy is based.

Whilst I am not a scientist, I gather that research is continuing, but it is looking like the conclusions of modern science are leading towards compatibility with those of the mystics of both ancient and modern times, to the effect that everything is interlinked, united, and ultimately part of a whole. All *is* one, as is illustrated by the non-dual philosopher Darryl Reanney in his book *Music of the Mind*, where he says:

> *This principle of separation is partly the legacy of science's attempts to place an intentional distance between observer and observed. The idea that human beings can experiment with nature in such a way that the experimenter does not influence the outcome of the experiment lies at the core of the scientific method; it is the basis of the doctrine of objectivity. Yet the whole testimony (of this book), the inner message of quantum physics, is that observer and observed, knower and known, are inseparably linked, resonating together in the shared song of knowing.*[4]

So where does that leave our page? And for that matter you and me? Well, we can perhaps reappraise our analysis from the other direction. Every *thing* is just a name and form by way of being an attribute of something bigger and more complex. And that bigger and more complex entity is just a name and form of an even bigger and more complex *thing*. This analytical process is leading slowly but surely to some surprising conclusions. Nothing is quite what it seems.

And in the last resort, this process tells us that there can only be but *one* real and definitive entity. And how can that conclusion not include you and me? We are simply parts of the whole. And that whole is incapable of being defined, segregated, or analysed. It may simply be referred to as the ultimate absolute non-dual reality. So the so-called individuals reading/

writing this *as individuals* (little I) are but part of the play of creation, whereas as big I, or the true self, we *are* that ultimate, absolute, non-dual reality.

Another way of apprehending this most important and significant concept is by considering a range of pots or cans full of water positioned outside in direct orientation from the sunlight. All reflect light from the sun. The sun always shines its light. The light in the cans can only exist with the sun's light. Without the light from the sun, there can be no light in the cans. The light in one can is in every way identical with the light in all the other cans, and the light in the sun itself. And that is how it is for us.

The Absolute, non-dual reality is symbolised by the sun. The individual being, whose existence and reality is totally dependent upon the Absolute, is symbolised by the individual rays of sunlight illuminating each can, so symbolising the self of each of us ("the light that lighteth every man coming into the world," as St John puts it). The can symbolises the individual body/ mind of each individual. Our journey, therefore, is to realise this to be so, that there can be no difference between, no separation from, and total unity with the sun and the sunlight. We can, therefore, now proceed to consider how this has been achieved around human civilisations around the globe, both spatially and temporally, which is how part II will now proceed.

PART 2

MINDFUL PHILOSOPHY: THE WHERE

INTRODUCTION

Now that we have some ideas about mindful philosophy and non-duality, which is part and parcel of the mindful approach, I think it would be helpful at this stage to give the theory some tests in practice. It seems to be believed in many cases that a good theory is all very well, but would be unlikely to work in practice. A theoretician is away with the fairies, but the practical man, trusting in common sense, has his feet on the ground and doesn't need fancy theories. Well, I don't think so.

These two stances aren't mutually exclusive. In fact, they are a good illustration of how one can approach life in dualistic mode (either theory or practicality) or in non-dualistic mode (*both* theory *and* practicality). A good theory cannot be good unless it works in practice. So let us now apply the principles of mindful philosophy to various traditions and cultures.

It can be seen just from this small example how duality, if seen for what it is, can lead to unity. The aim is to take a look at where in creation this has been found to be useful, and so potentially capable of throwing new light on old traditions. We may find in consideration of many of the world's great religions and wisdom traditions that a similar result will arise—from apparent duality there can arise the actuality of unity. That said, duality in this manner need not be derided—in fact, it needs to be seen as an inevitable and, indeed, essential tool, the ultimate fulfilment of which is unity, or non-duality.

We will start in chapter 3 by considering the tradition probably closest to the hearts and minds of the Western world, that of Christianity. I am including within this section of the book the Neoplatonists, and the teachings of the great Italian renaissance guide, Marsilio Ficino. This is because there is an overlap within these teachings, and Christianity as is now recorded is undoubtedly influenced by Platonic/Neoplatonic thought. To comprehend the latter two, a glance at Socrates and Plato would be useful from the perspective of non-duality, together with the teachings of luminaries such as Plotinus. We will then move on in chapter 4 to consider how non-dual teachings have influenced a number of other Western traditions, including Gnosticism, teachings from Egypt, and indeed from what are referred to as "pagan" sources. I am also including a brief insight into Sufism (the mystical side to Islam) at this stage.

Chapter 5 covers data from the Far East, with which the non-dual tradition is more commonly associated, notably from certain areas of Buddhism, Taoism, and elsewhere. We expand this in chapter 6 by a consideration of the Advaita Vedanta tradition from India, which arguably is presently having the most significant influence in the Western world. We will then be having a brief look at other areas where non-duality can be discerned, such as Ubuntu in Africa, teachings from Australasia, and the native Americans and others. We also look at modern non-dual teachers and teachings, including Neo-Advaita, and the place of myth and legend to help us on our way towards comprehension of what can be quite challenging ideas and concepts.

In chapter 8, we will consider more modern illustrations, including what is sometimes known as the perennial philosophy, together with the transcendentalist tradition in the United States, and the influence of theosophy, notably by way of the teacher Krishnamurti. Finally, to conclude part 2, we examine the data coming out of contemporary science and research.

CHAPTER 3

CHRISTIANITY, THE PLATONIC TRADITION, AND NON-DUALITY

When you make the two one, and when you make the inner as the

outer and the outer as the inner and the above as the below, and

when you make the male and the female into a single one, then

shall you enter the kingdom.

These words were spoken by Jesus Christ as reported in the Gnostic Gospel of St Thomas, being one of a number of scripts taken from the Nag Hammadi scrolls discovered in Egypt in 1945. They constitute one of the most succinct and direct pieces of teaching from Jesus, and form an ideal platform to consider non-duality within the Christian tradition.

What is meant by the words "the Kingdom"? This is a reference to the kingdom of heaven, which had been placed by Jesus in another conversation as "being within", and in yet another discussion in St Thomas's gospel as being "within and without you". This is a realised state of union with the Divine. It is something that can be perceived cutting across the wisdom traditions of the world, including the attainment of nirvana in the Buddhist tradition, and self-realisation under Advaita Vedanta from India, which is particularly graphic because it basically reveals that the goal is realisation of the true self in all of us, as outlined in the four precepts.

Then there are references in Buddhism to attaining one's "Buddha nature", or the Buddha within, and in the Psalms, there are various references, including, "Ye too are Gods, sons of the most high", and, "Be still, and know that I am (God)." In other words, through deep stillness, the knowledge that ultimately we are all essentially Divine is made manifest.

Jesus and Non-Duality

The St Thomas quote, then, is an exhortation to us to "enter the kingdom", and gives a number of examples as to how this might be done. To "make the two one" is a composite direction to see unity rather than division. The temptation in modern life is always to see things as alternatives rather than as being complimentary. So we can consider liberalism or conservatism, masculinity or femininity, left or right, up or down, tall or short, intellect or intuition, deep or shallow, black or white, good or bad, and so on. The list can get longer and longer.

But to follow the advice of Jesus, there is the possibility of putting on one side our innate preferences about these opposing ideas. It is a question of letting go. To let go means to relinquish our claim on one or other of the alternatives and so see them as they really are, not as we would like them to be, or think they ought to be. And in that freedom, we can see that there is a bigger picture.

There is always a bigger picture, but it is so often covered up by the concerns of the ego, or little I, to implement its priorities. This bigger picture is, of course, the essence of the situation. If we are continually being offered either one side of the coin or the other, it is very difficult in such circumstances to remember the actual coin—we forget there is a coin at all. And that's the point—the coin is what is discovered, metaphorically speaking, when we approach life's choices with the unitive, non-dual approach.

The quote continues with other examples: making the inner as the outer and the outer as the inner, and the above as the below. So if we are being true to ourselves, we can manifest outwardly what is going on inwardly. This means that either we need to exercise great care about what is going on inwardly, or, if we wish to present a civilised appearance we will have to exhibit a false appearance or facade. Also, to make the above as the below is similarly a direction to attend to what is motivating us—the intention behind the action.

So it is easy to see Jesus as a teacher of the highest stature. This is not the place to discuss his Divine and pre-eminent status, that is, entering the field of religious analysis. But viewed from the perspective of non-duality, it can be seen that all human beings contain within them the Divine essence.

And that Divine essence is unlimited, and without causality, is undefinable and immutable. As such, it provides the link between us and one another, and us and Jesus or any other teacher.

In the opening verses of St John's gospel, there is a reference to the "true light, which lighteth every man coming into the world". This Divine essence is that light. So if St John is to be believed, this light illuminates *every* man (i.e., all humanity, female as well as male). So you do not need to be a member of a particular grouping or religion, or to adopt any particular creed or belief system. These words were written before there was a church, or any kind of religious establishment, and were meant to be heard inclusively and not as the exclusive property of any particular organisation. They therefore exemplify the non-dual and universal aspect to what became to be known as the Christian teaching.

There is a strong tradition in the Christian way of offering two modes of existence. They comprise the alternatives of the active life, or the contemplative life. This again has the potential to seem dualistic, and inevitably up to a point is. The contemplative life is often considered to be the province of monks, ascetics, and those drawn to an existence of withdrawal from the path followed by the ordinary householder and family member. One can comprehend and, as it were, merge with the Divine in an environment conducive to peace and quiet to enable meditation, contemplation, and reflection to fructify. These are the highest goals available to humanity, and the contemplative provides to the householder a Divine and holy example of how life can be led devoid of material concerns, the aims of which are solely those of spirituality.

This is exemplified in the tale of Mary and Martha where, according to Luke chapter 10, Jesus had been welcomed to the house of Martha, whose sister, Mary, sat and listened to what he had to say. But Martha was "distracted by her many tasks" and ultimately became so upset by the non-contribution of her sister to the jobs on hand that she complained to Jesus, "Do you not care that my sister has left me to get on with the work by myself? Tell her to come and lend a hand." Well, she did not get the answer she was expecting because all he said was, "Martha, Martha, you are fretting and fussing about so many things, but one thing is necessary. The part that Mary has chosen is best, and it shall not be taken away from her."

So Jesus was apparently extolling the virtues of simply being still and listening over busying about doing lots of "stuff". Now it is inconceivable that the stuff will not, in due process, get done. And Jesus didn't decry that. But in that precise situation, was it really so important given the opportunity to hear the words of the master? And is there not a huge lesson here for us in the twenty-first century in which the massive advance of technology, ostensibly making life easier with more time for leisure activities and rest, is creating precisely the opposite? It is now normal for people to feel they have to engage with their mobile phones in the small hours of the morning, at mealtimes, during conversations with friends and family, and at every hour of day and night. We are stuff-driven. And do we feel the better for it? If not, then what is the alternative?

The contemplative life is exemplified by Mary, who took the better path, and the active life by Martha with all her fretting and fussing. Viewed from the perspective of non-duality, it is not a case of *either* the active life *or* the contemplative life, but *both/and*. The active life in this way can be seen as a preparation for the contemplative life, which does not exclude action as such. It simply places it in context and allows it to take place not as an end in itself, but with detachment so far as the end result is concerned, or in terms as to how the action and one's attitude to it is performed. Jesus simply and directly made it quite clear that a measure and a balance are needed.

Similar advice was given in the Sermon on the Mount. In mindfulness and non-dual philosophy much is made of the need to be present, be in the moment, and "in the now". The issues that preclude this being availed are desires, fears, fantasies, and the like, which occupy the mind and which are the exclusive province of little I, the ego.

Plainly, not much has changed since the time of Jesus, if Matthew is to be believed. In chapter 6, verses 25-31, he is reported as advising,

I bid you put away anxious thoughts about food and drink to keep
you alive, and clothes to cover your body. Surely life is more than
food, the body more than clothes. Look at the birds of the air; they
do not sow and reap and store in barns, yet your heavenly Father
feeds them. You are worth more than birds! ... Consider how the
lilies grow in the fields; they do not work, they do not spin; and yet
I tell you not even Solomon in all his splendour was attired like one
of these. But if that is how God clothes the grass in the fields, which
is there today, and tomorrow thrown into the stove, will he not all
the more clothe you, Oh you of little faith. (New English Bible)

Ultimately he gives the advice "set your mind on God's kingdom and his justice before everything else, and all the rest will come to you as well. Do not be anxious about tomorrow, tomorrow can look after itself. Each day has troubles enough of its own."

The moral to the tale is to realise that if we can but live in the present moment, we can experience the wondrous beauty of the world we inhabit. We do, however, need to trust that moment and to reorganise our priorities. It seems to be common ground that, by putting *truth* first, this subtly reorganises the dynamic of one's life and opens the gate to what is known as *grace* in the Christian tradition (and *punya* and the Indian).

Jesus is not advocating a process of unintelligent or wilful negligence, and certainly one needs at all times to retain basic common sense about practicalities. There is an earthy quote from the Islam tradition which advises, "Put your trust in God—but first tie up your camel." What is, however, being recommended is a review of what we put first. In the non-dual tradition, we can do that by simply coming into the moment so that the mind with all its thoughts can quieten, which will allow us to actually see what lies before us and so meet the need of the moment without being influenced by egoic ideas of preference or aversion. After all, that's what every parent inevitably has to engage with when dealing with young children, do they not?

Jesus was asked a question, again in the gospel according to St Thomas: "Tell us how our end will be?" I suspect the answer may have surprised them, because it is really an exhortation to really live in the moment and be fully present: "Have you then discovered the beginning so that you inquire about the end? For where the beginning is, there shall be the end. Blessed is he who shall stand at the beginning, and he shall know the end, and he shall not taste death." This sounds remarkably familiar as it might have been written by T. S. Eliot, who refers to this timelessness quality of true presence in the lines:

> *We shall not cease from exploration*
> *And the end of all of our exploring*
> *Will be to arrive where we started*
> *And know the place for the first time.*
>
> T. S. Eliot, "Little Gidding"

A further question was put to Jesus by a lawyer who wanted to know which of the Ten Commandments was the most important. Jesus answered, "The most important is, 'Hear, Oh Israel; The Lord our God is One. Love the Lord your God with all your heart, with all your soul, with all your mind, and with all your strength'" and to "love your neighbour as yourself."

So this not only reminds us of unity, or non-duality, but also introduces the notion of love. Viewed from the perspective of non-duality, this is of great interest because it is not a question of loving one's neighbour as if they were me, but loving him or her as *the* Self. In other words, this is another instance where universal principles are at work. What comes out of this is the fact that love by its nature in unlimited if it is allowed to manifest in its pure, ego-free form. We will be looking at this in greater depth in chapter 10, but for now the message is that if love is unlimited, how could it be other than universal? So the Divine can be perceived in all beings in this way—the Supreme Being immanent throughout the whole of creation.

A similar situation is illustrated in the injunction to "love your enemies" and to "turn the other cheek". I believe that it is only by taking a universal approach to the particular incident that it is possible to raise our game, and in so doing the duality of me and enemy become alchemised to Self and self. And this is the point—it is precisely what mindful philosophy is about. The famous but enigmatic phrase from Exodus that God is reported to have stated in the tale of the burning bush that *"I am that I am"* is telling the same tale. This tale is quite simply that when all is said and done there is nothing but *Self*, and that the Self is the ultimate non-dual reality of us all, and of everything. "I am" is a statement of absolute truth. It must, therefore, follow that it is wholly inconceivable to state with any conviction "I am not". After all, who is it who is doing the speaking?

The Christian message is proffered in many guises today, and it is good to know that the non-dual perspective is included in this. The well-known guide Richard Rohr has written on this, and draws the distinction between what he calls one's *false* self and one's *true* Self. The false self is a social and mental construct to get you started on your life journey. In one of his daily meditations, he describes it as "a set of agreements between you and your parents, your family, your school chums, your partner or spouse, your culture, and your religion." He goes on to explain that it is defined by being distinguished and separate from others, necessary to start things off but, if one does not move beyond it, becoming a source of increasing problems as life goes on. It's what, he reminds us, Jesus refers to as one's "wineskin"—or container—all well and good to contain good new wine, but which will ultimately decay and burst so that both wine and container are lost. The recommendation is that growth and change are needed; we need to move away from the old, suspect wineskin, and move out of the control of the false self because of its limitations. At the right time in our development, we will emerge into the light of our true selves, in the process of which we will disempower our false self and not feel that anything has been lost.

The alternative is to remain stuck and trapped in a false, constricted, and fear-driven world driven only by considerations of "me and mine".

Non-duality is alive and well today within the Christian teaching, as exemplified by Rohr and by the teachings of John Main, who spent time in India before promoting the mantra-based Christian meditation technique which is continued by his successor, Father Lawrence Freeman. There is now an organisation known as the World Council of Christian Meditation which exists to make available, within a Christian context, the type of meditation practices that the Hesychasts used (Orthodox Christian mystics—see below), and that which is to be found within Eastern traditions. Perhaps the most well-known exponent of this "marriage of East and West" is the late Dom Bede Griffiths, who wrote a book of that name, who spent time living in an ashram in India, and whose life journey was to make available to his followers the simple truth that there are no differences between East and West, and that what we all need is to remove ourselves from the duality of such opposites, including intellect and intuition, male and female, black and white, and the like, all as stated in the quote from Jesus which heads up this chapter. Here is a sample of his teaching from his book *The Universal Christ*:

> *Christianity came out of the Semitic world of Jewish culture.*
> *Its teaching, definitions and thought were largely formed by*
> *Greek culture and philosophy. For nearly two thousand years the*
> *movement of the Church has been westwards.*

55

The twentieth century has witnessed a powerful convergence of Western and Eastern cultures and this is profoundly affecting today's Church. Meditation, once thought to be the prerogative of Eastern and non-Christian religions, has thus opened the door into a Christ—centred spirituality for thousands of Westerners.

The immanent or indwelling God always central to Eastern spirituality is now by many seen to be at one with the Pauline doctrine of "Christ in you, the hope of glory" (Ephesians 3).

God is one. Knowledge of the one God comes to all human beings through the opening of the heart. This is the true ecumenism. It is the true interior religion of Christ for which today there is great yearning.

Plato, Socrates, and the Greek Tradition

Socrates, or Plato reciting his teachings, is referred to by some as the master philosopher of the Western world. Quite obviously, teaching as he was some four hundred years before Jesus, he cannot be described as Christian. However, his powerful words, including his references to a single supreme being, convinced many philosophers in the first and second centuries after Christ that in some way his teachings needed to be integrated into those of the embryonic Christian church.

Socrates wrote nothing his own, and what we have today by way of a number of books or "dialogues", including *The Republic, The Laws, Timaeus, Phaedo,* and so on are courtesy of his pupil and scribe, Plato. His presence in this book is really by way of what seems to have been an approach to living aimed at "the Good". The Good was the supreme "idea". This is the logical conclusion from the notion that it is the idea, or form, behind an item wherein its reality is to be perceived, rather than its manifestation. "The Good" is symbolised by the light in the sun, and life should be lived in a self-enquiring manner, and humans need to live and comply with certain Platonic virtues or goods—human goods and Divine goods. He held that there were such things as absolute truth, justice, and beauty.

This might seem contentious today, but by taking a unitive approach based upon the spiritual non-dual essence of humankind, which he referred to as the soul, which herself (he used the feminine gender to describe the soul because in his view the feminine approach was saintlier) reflected spirituality (which he referred to as the One, or the Monad, or the Source). In this way he was able to articulate an idealist lifestyle and an idealist manner of governance, in so doing infusing the stuff of everyday life with a spiritual or unitive perspective. That's why the Socratic/Platonic tradition can find a worthy place in any analysis of non-duality. Such was the power of his teaching that he inspired many leading lights such as Plotinus in the third century to Marsilio Ficino in the fifteenth, collectively known as the Neoplatonists. Some consider Shakespeare to have been influenced in these areas.

One of the principle ways Plato found favour with the early Christians was by way of his guidance on the notion of beauty. He regarded beauty as Divine:

> *But what if man had eyes to see the true beauty—the divine beauty, I mean pure and clear and unalloyed, not clogged with the pollution of mortality and all the colours and vanities of human life—gazing upon it in communion with the true beauty simple and divine; remember how in that communion only, beholding beauty with the eye of the mind, he will be able to bring forth not shadows of beauty, but its truth, because it is no shadow that he grasps, but the truth. And he will give birth to true virtue and nourish it, and become a friend of the One, and be immortal as far as mortal man may.*

His concept of beauty is here revealed as incorporating truth and immortality, perceived only by way of "the eye of the mind". For Socrates there was only ever *one* beauty. Whenever beauty is recognised, be it the physical beauty of a wondrous sunset, the sensual beauty of art and architecture, or the subtle beauty of fine ideas, standards of behaviour and aspirations, it is all one. A single beauty absolute, not myriads of individual beauties reflected through each item of creation. The immortal lines of the nineteenth-century English poet John Keats which appear at the end of his poem "Ode to a Grecian Urn" seem to emanate from the same source of Divine inspiration: "Beauty is truth, truth beauty, that is all ye know on earth, and all ye need to know."

In the "Symposium", there is a passage in which Socrates reveals how Diotima, a wise teacher, instructed her students about the spiritual aspect of beauty:

> *He who has been instructed thus far in the things of love, and who has learned to see the beautiful in due order and succession, when he comes towards the end will suddenly perceive a nature of wondrous beauty—a nature which in the first place is everlasting, knowing not birth or death, growth or decay; secondly not fair in one point of view or foul in another ... but beauty absolute, existing within itself, simple and everlasting, which is imparted to the ever growing and perishing beauties of all other beautiful things, without itself suffering diminution, or increase, or any change.*

From this quote from Diotima, it is clear that the implications of this are profound and plainly centred around the non-dual essence which was described in precept one, and because it shines throughout "all other beautiful things" does not exclude us—you and me. That is what is referred to in precept two.

This general direction of travel to be found in the works of Plato and Socrates is perhaps expressed more fully and clearly in the famous allegory of The Cave. This is a tale of human beings, bound by chains to a chair, in such a way that they can only view the back of the cave. They have no notion of what goes on at the front of the cave or beyond, because their reality (or what was "true for them") is dependent solely upon what they can perceive. But behind them lies the exit, approached apparently by a "steep and rugged ascent", beyond which there is a permanent brazier burning away in front of which is a raised roadway upon which ordinary life is taking place—human artefacts of every type being carried this way and that, partially concealed by a low wall. But all the prisoners can see are shadows reflected from the light from the fire upon the wall in front of them.

Now it transpires that one of these prisoners is freed, then conducted to the exit, under instruction. He has a tough time, distressed at first, but ultimately comprehending the wonder of what was happening when compared to the shadowland which was his former state. Finally, he is confronted with the sun itself, then dazzled, but eventually appreciating the light and how shadows are caused by the light reflecting the artefacts—a quite different view to that upon which his former view of reality had been based. Upon acclimatisation his wonderment increases. But there comes a time when he must return to his chained chair. To get there, he needs to acclimatise to the increasingly dark conditions. Upon reaching his colleagues, he is quite unable to describe in a coherent state what he had found—indeed, his friends thought he had gone mad. And when he tried to get them to understand the true nature of reality as it had been revealed to him, they thought he had lost his senses and were all the more convinced of the wisdom of staying put—far too much at risk to go exploring.

This is a profound allegory, one of the most graphic descriptions of how non-dual teaching works. The small, limited world of apparent reality is a reference to what can be our habit-driven and limited materialist world. The chains that bind us to it are many and various, but to the non-dual philosopher are things that create duality—like fears, desires, and aversions, and all the panoply of little I, or the ego. Once they are severed, however, given appropriate instruction, we can start to appreciate reality in all its fullness.

This is what Plato means by "the idea of Good". This idea is "seen only with an effort; although when seen, it is inferred to be the universal author of all things beautiful and right, parent of right and lord of light in the visible world, and the immediate and supreme source of reason and truth in the intellectual; and that this is the power upon which he who would act rationally either in public or private life must have his eyes fixed".

And that reality is universally glorious, available to all, and constitutes "absolute truth"—not the limiting and constricting notion of "true for me".

Neoplatonists and Others

Plotinus

Realised human beings, according to Plotinus, "see all things, not in the process of becoming, but in Being, and see themselves in the other. Each being contains in him/herself in the other. Therefore, All is everywhere. Each is there All, and All is each. Man as he now is has ceased to be the All. But when he ceases to be an individual, he raises himself again and penetrates the whole world."

The power of the teachings of Plato/Socrates had a profound effect upon the philosophies of successive cultures, including that of Islam, and Socrates is quoted in Gnostic and Jewish literature also. What is now called paganism used these teachings. Neo- and Midplatonism were forces which ebbed and flowed from the AD 400s to the so-called Age of Reason, and there is every reason to suppose that Shakespeare fell under such influences to greater or lesser extent.

One of the first and most influential of the Neoplatonic philosophers was the Alexandrian spiritual teacher, Plotinus, who lived in the third century BCE. He himself had many followers, and much of what we know about him is due to writings of his student, Porphyry. He produced a series of six enneads, or treatises upon various aspects of philosophy. He was influenced by Egyptian and Eastern esoteric philosophy. He saw the make-up of the human being as emanating from the Supreme: "So it is with us: it is from the Supreme that we derive order, and distribution, and harmony."

He used the idea of soul and "essential soul," and he wrote that evil occurs when the soul is associated with the body. Purification is the process of throwing off to reveal one's state of "intellectation and wisdom" in order to revert to our innate "goodness". That which emerges is "the Good", reminiscent of Plato. The soul is a derivative of "the One", which is a supreme essence devoid of any attributes and so transcends creation.

He goes on to suggest that creation evolves from the One, by way of various emanations, in progressively reduced states of perfection, the first of which is the "Logos", or "Nous", via the human and animal kingdoms, to matter. But because everything comes from the One, it is all divinely infused, or, to put it another way, the divine is immanent throughout all creation. This is an indication of non-duality and is well illustrated by the quotation heading up this section.

Also, in the next quotation is a reference to "the All", which is stated to integrate "all living beings". So, it is difficult to avoid the basic conclusion that Plotinus, who had both many teachings from both East and West influencing and formulating his views, had a view that unity was what was underlying everything in and beyond the manifest creation, and that the destiny of man is to realise this unity:

> *This All is one universally comprehensive living being, encircling all the living beings within it and having a soul, one soul, which extends to all its members; every separate thing is an integral part of this All by belonging to the total material fabric, while, in so far as it has participation in the All—Soul, it possesses spiritual membership as well. Each separate thing is affected none the less by all else in virtue of the common participation in the All.*

The Orthodox Tradition

Moving back to the Christian teaching as it began to take shape, one can discern the embryonic Christian monastic tradition within what became known as the "desert fathers" and "desert mothers". Commencing in the third century, a group of ascetics set up a monastic and reclusive mode of living in the Arabian desert under the tutelage (initially) of St Anthony the Great. They adopted lifestyles of complete renunciation of worldly pleasures, taking up austerity and solitude in order to provide an appropriate ambience to cultivate inner peace and contemplation. From this was generated the monastic tradition which came to fruition in the West (including the "rule of St Benedict"). In the East, following the demise of the Roman Empire and the subsequent division of the Christian church into two centres, the Roman Catholic in the West and the Orthodox in the East, based in Constantinople, there developed the monastic tradition of the Hesychasts.

The Hesychasts are of particular interest from the perspective of non-duality. Hesychasm basically means stillness, or quietness. The Orthodox churches do retain a particular aura of spirituality in many areas even today. This may be on account partially of the tradition within which the Hesychasts played an important formative role in the early Middle Ages, and also on account of the careful preparation and use, by highly skilled and spiritual teachers, of icons. Viewing an icon in such circumstances could bring the viewer into direct contact with the relevant archetype, and a feeling of Divine union. The Hesychasts laid great emphasis similarly upon mysticism. Prayer and contemplation were of paramount importance, notably the Jesus Prayer, or prayer of the heart, as they referred to it. The Jesus Prayer is essentially an invocation to the dispelling of ignorance and the acquisition of illumination.

In due course, the traditions of the Hesychasts were encoded within a collection of readings and works known as the Philokalia which saw publication in 1782. It comprised a compendium of spiritual teachings from the third century onwards. Stillness and inner tranquillity were the goals. They took the view that, to come to peace and stillness, what was of supreme importance was control over the movements of the mind. To effect this, they took measures to replace the day-to-day thoughts and mental processes by repetition in the mind of a suitable spiritual passage, or expression of truth, such as the Jesus Prayer. The practice, known as *nepsis*, could be thus described as a form of contemplative prayer, but having an element of detachment through which the intellect was purified, refined, and perfected.

Nepsis is a Greek word which means "watchfulness" and, because of the need to watch one's thoughts, desires, motivations, and the like, can be likened to what is today called mindfulness. It is more like meditation as is understood in today's parlance. This practice is continued today on a much wider basis by way of a form of mantra-style meditation which, courtesy of luminaries such as the John Main and Father Lawrence Freeman, has become of global significance.

The Philokalia also provided advice upon practices conducive to inner peace, such as breath control. The point of this direction of travel was that if there is to be any comprehension of the Divine, then it is not the mind that is required. It is simply not possible to describe the Absolute Being. One can state what he, she, or it is not (the "via negativa"—the way of negation), but it is not possible, other than by way of Divine union, to state positively what the Divine actually is. So by stilling the mind, the Hesychasts took the view that there could be some kind of understanding by way of inner peace, which had a universal quality devoid of data from the mind, sense objects, or reasoned analysis.

Whilst the Hesychasts took an approach that was not without controversy, the upshot seems to have been that the Philokalia became integrated as a mystical and highly important part of the Orthodox tradition. And this is, it seems to me, of some significance to the mindful philosophy student. There is much that is common ground between Hesychant watchfulness and modern-day mindfulness, together with the Mahayana Buddhist teaching, Advaita Vedanta, and others, and so exemplifies a continuation of the thread of non-duality contained in all genuinely mystical traditions.

Quite obviously, there is use of Christian nomenclature, but this should not disguise the fact that enwrapped within the Christian teaching lies a tradition of meditation, contemplation, and spiritual unity. This is pure non-duality—it is in effect telling us that the ultimate Divine essence is simply concealed by a veil of illusion (like the Maya as described in the Bhagavad Gita in the Indian teaching). And that veil of illusion is unreal.

Aquinas, Eckhart, Ficino

During the Middle Ages, there was a flowering of spiritual thought and philosophy due to a resurgence of Neoplatonic influences and the works of Pythagoras and Aristotle. Philosophers who were thus inspired include Thomas Aquinas, an Italian medieval priest and scholar. He was responsible for integrating the thinking of Aristotle and Socrates with Plato into Christian culture. He believed that access to the Divine could be attained using human reason, in the process of which he issued five positive considerations indicating how, with reason, we can comprehend the nature of the Divine. (God is simple, perfect, infinite, immutable and One). He issued a treatise called "Quinquae Viae" ("Five Ways") in which he argues that the existence of God can be proven and is self-evident.

These arguments caused him much tribulation, running, as they did, contrary to the doctrines of the Church of Rome which was to the effect that the will of God transcended human reason, which was an inappropriate methodology for Divine understanding. However, despite being accused of heresy and ultimately being posthumously condemned, his works resonate with a more modern readership, and certainly there is something of a universal approach about his teaching, for if there are, as he advised, two basic pathways towards Divine comprehension, faith and reason, surely every man and woman can have access to these because they are clearly to be found to greater or lesser extent lodged in all of us.

Aquinas was on two occasions employed at the University of Paris where he wrote his famous "Summa Theologiae", and after his death in 1274, his condemnation in 1277, ultimately was restored by the Catholic Church and was canonised in 1323. In 1879, Pope Leo XIII declared his work to comprise "the only true philosophy", and his influence thereafter is of the greatest significance to those of the Christian persuasion who take a full and inclusive approach to the universal teachings of Jesus.

The Socratic/Platonic way casts a long and undimmed beam of light into Western culture, particularly as integrated to no small extent into Christian teaching. The thirteenth-century German mystic Meister Eckhart took the view that the Trinity, or tripartite Godhead, was not comprehensible and undefinable. It did, however, manifest in the soul of human beings, and thus permeated all humanity—a very non-dual notion. He had an almost Buddhist-like stance on the ultimate reality: "One should love God as not-God, not-Spirit, not-person, not-image, but as he is, a sheer, pure absolute One, sundered from all two-ness, and in whom we must eternally sink from nothingness to nothingness."

This is very close to the Buddhist notion of "suchness", or the Void, as all endeavours to describe the indescribable must ultimately fail. He was able to comprehend the universality of the Divine and took the view that to have any understanding of that, one has somehow to merge, or become one with it: "Whoever has God in mind, simply and solely God, in all things, such a man carries God with him into all his works and into all places, and God alone does all his works. He seeks nothing but God, nothing seems good to him but God. He becomes one with God in every thought. Just as no multiplicity can dissipate God, so nothing can dissipate this man or make him multiple."

So the golden thread of non-duality, or the Socratic beam of light, runs clearly and fully throughout the Christian mystical tradition, wherein despite all manner of clerical and establishment pressures, the truth was made plain by great men such as Eckhart, Aquinas, and others.

This beam of light was markedly enhanced in fifteenth-century Florence, when one Marsilio Ficino (1433-99), was employed by Cosimo de Medici to realise his new-found enthusiasm for the recently rediscovered Plato by translating him from Greek into Latin. Ficino was a philosopher/priest. He was inspired by Plato's teachings, establishing a Platonic academy in Florence. This academy was attended by many of the Florentine "greats", and was the inspiration for a wondrous collection of luminaries including Michelangelo, Raphael, Botticelli, and Titian. Inscribed around its walls were the following words: "All things are directed from goodness to goodness. Rejoice in the present. Set no value on property. Seek no honours. Avoid excess. Avoid (unnecessary) activity. Rejoice in the present."

This sounds like a modern mindfulness injunction, and its emphasis upon the present moment resonates deeply with the mindful approach which our discipline of mindful or non-dual philosophy is promulgating. And within one of his letters is contained the following advice:

> *If we wish to attain what we are seeking, to flee only to that which does not flee anywhere … is there any need to be moved to that which does not move anywhere, which is present everywhere in every single thing? Then let us not be moved or distracted by many things, but let us remain in unity as much as we are able, since we find eternal unity and the one eternity not through movement or multiplicity, but by being still and being one. But what is that one, friends? Is it not that self same good which fills the universe?*

So we have in this short piece a reference to non-duality, this being realisable, for it is essentially what we are, by the mindfulness practice of letting the mind come to stillness (not being moved or distracted, etc.). The reference to attain what we are seeking is the goal of all true philosophy— to come to a true understanding of what and who we really are. And the outcome is the "self same good" that fills the universe.

This is a highly Platonic take on things, and can also be said to have Gnostic overtones, for reasons that will become apparent later. Ficino, in this passage, has outlined thereby the point and purpose of mindful philosophy, which is the fulfilment of the inscription over the Delphic oracle to "Know Thyself", something dear to the heart of Gnosticism, where we will turn to next.

CHAPTER 4

GNOSTICISM, HERMETICISM, AND THE SUFIS

Running through the Middle East at a similar time to the early Neoplatonists were a number of spiritual traditions. They vary greatly, but there does seem to be a thread linking them, and whilst at the time this may not have been apparent to them, it seems that the multicoloured and infinitely varied thread (in terms of manifestation) of non-duality ran throughout these schools of thought. They comprise the Hermetic tradition from ancient Egypt, reinvigorated by Marsilio Ficino as part of the Neoplatonist direction, the Sufis from Persia and the Islam world, and the Gnostics, who, for reasons more to do with power politics than philosophical improvement, virtually disappeared from sight for the best part of 1,500 years. As far as the Gnostics are concerned, because of their low profile and that until recently not a lot was known about them, I will perhaps delve a little deeper into the background here than I have elsewhere. These traditions ran in parallel with the Christian church, and in the spirit of non-duality, it is interesting to reflect the extent at one stage, in the pre-Crusade era, that there appears to have been something of a cross-fertilisation of ideas to some degree.

These traditions interfaced with each other, and much of the terminology, such as words like *gnosis, andropos,* and *logos* crop up from time to time in all of them to greater or lesser extent. These words are of Greek extraction, illustrating the huge influence the Greek tradition, notably Pythagoras, and later Socrates and Plato, had on all these traditions. The aim of putting them together here is that, by using mindful philosophy techniques, it is possible to discern much common ground of a non-dual character. This includes the notion that there is no differentiation between the true essence of human beings and the source, and that what we might refer to as the *soul* of humans, or higher mind (as opposed to spirit), can be manifested in a threefold option: base or material bound, a state of evolution (albeit there is always the choice of the direction of evolution), and spiritual unity. This implies that ultimately there will be realisation of the true spiritual composition of us all, which is a state of unity.

One does come across the notion of "mysteries" in all these teachings. The ancient Egyptian civilisation was the most ancient of these traditions, and used the concept of a Divine trinity, Osiris(male), Isis (female), and Horus to help the aspirant realise these "mysteries" and so comprehend the truth about himself or herself. This was closely resembled in the pagan/Gnostic practice, in which the Trinity comprised God the mother (Sofia, goddess of wisdom), God the father, or the Monad/the Good, and in Christian Gnosticism, God the Son. This was not something which was ultimately acceptable to what is now "establishment Christianity" (God the father,

God the son—Jesus, and God the Holy Spirit) but does illustrate the inclusion on equal terms in the ancient traditions of the female with the male.

The "mysteries" which were of so much importance to all these teachings are in relation to the need, according to Plato, not to simply rely upon opinion or faith, which is simply a belief system (*dexa*), just relating to the appearance of things. For full reliance, one needs knowledge (*epistome*), which is that which permeates and acts as substratum to the world of opinion and belief. Only by the practice of philosophy can that desirable goal be attained. And it was done so across these pathways by virtue of a deep and carefully designed "road map" designed to lead the aspirant (who is basically you and me, for these purposes) from a state of ignorance and bondage, via enlightenment, and ultimately initiation into full unitive essence. The "mysteries" are simply the identification that such a path does exist, and that is as true today as it was then. Such precious and esoteric knowledge needed the utmost care in its dissemination, so great discrimination was required as to who, and under what circumstances, such truths were to be imparted—in other words, to allow the exoteric to become esoteric.

Gnosticism

The Gnostics were a somewhat disparate grouping, and probably never formed a cohesive group at all. There are Christian Gnostics, Egyptian or Hermetic Gnostics, and Jewish Gnostics. These spawned a number of groupings and subgroupings, so coming to any doctrinal conclusions is difficult. Add to this the fact that after reaching a "high point" in the second century CE, their influence suddenly waned, and after losing influence within the Roman establishment after the adoption by Rome of what became establishment Christianity, they were ruthlessly persecuted.

It is the victors who write the history books, so what we now know about them is derived to no small extent from the records of their detractors, which does not make for a particularly balanced or unbiased view. However, given that there does seem to be a renewal of interest in this important plank of the Western spiritual tradition, at this stage I would like to offer a few thoughts within the context of this appraisal of non-duality, in the interests of redressing the balance.

So what was it about the Gnostics that was so inimical to the church establishment, both then and upon numerous times subsequently, including the notorious Albigensian campaign in Languedoc in the early thirteenth century which finally and horrifically did away with the Cathars (possible Gnostic-influenced Christians)? Why was the church so riddled with fear? What is it about the Gnostic path that somehow transcended the trials and tribulations with which it was inflicted for a thousand years, so much so that strands of Gnostic-based thought and teaching permeated many European teachings and influenced many scholars? And why are the Gnostics being featured in a book on non-duality? Let's start at the beginning.

Origins

No one seems to know how the Gnostics started. What we do know is that the common thread running through their history right up to the present day is the notion of *gnosis*. Gnosis can be translated as "higher knowledge". The English word *know* is derived from the Greek word *gnossos*. It would seem a fair bet that the Greeks derived their word, via unknown linkage, from the Sanskrit word *jnana*—again meaning "higher knowledge." Higher knowledge in this context may be contrasted with "lower" or "ordinary" knowledge. This is a simple accumulation of information.

This, however, does not constitute wisdom, which is only attainable via the acquisition of higher knowledge. This essentially means oneness with the Divine. It means knowledge of God. It means the comprehension of the Divine essence within us as human beings, and thereby attaining unity with that. And the only way such knowledge can be comprehended is by merging with it. Gnosis is the actual experience of the ultimate reality and the understanding of the context and significance of that experience. Research carried out by Tobias Churton in his book *Gnostic Philosophy* emphasises that gnosis is to be equated with the spiritual universal essence.[1] This essence is known as *Brahman* in the ancient Vedic tradition, which is of the same nature as the individual Self which I have referred to as *big I*, known in Vedic parlance as atman.

Churton came across a quote in one of the Nag Hammadi scrolls which appears to contain a straight quotation from the Katha Upanishad, stating, in the context of killing a human being, "He did not kill, nor was he killed."[2] This is a reference to the fact that to kill the physical body does not mean the killing of the spiritual essence of human beings. (This is not, of course, to condone such awful and catastrophic acts— just an endeavour to place them in context when viewed from a spiritual perspective.) Such statements appear similarly in the Bhagavad Gita and throughout the Vedic tradition, so it seems that the Gnostic notion of the ultimate reality being Divine and imperishable was a reflection of this teaching.

In the Vedic or Indian tradition, there are said to be three potential pathways to the Divine, or yogas. They are karma yoga, the way of action; bhakti yoga, the way of devotion (to which most religions dependent upon a personalised vision of the deity would subscribe); and *jnana* yoga, the way of higher knowledge. In my view, Gnosticism is a straight derivation of this last path, and it does seem remarkable, for reasons which will become apparent, that there seems to be a considerable overlap between non-duality in the Vedic tradition (Advaita Vedanta) and Gnosticism (like Christianity, of Middle Eastern origin but manifesting in the West). I have not been able to discern any direct link, and this view will not be found via the textbooks, but the end result is clear enough.

There is evidence that Gnosticism travelled from Zoroastrian sources in Persia by way of the Arabian cultures to emerge and interface with the embryo Christian church at the time of Christ and after. As has been said, there is very little documentary evidence, but in 1945 there came a substantial boon to the Gnostic repertoire. This was the discovery by a couple of local residents in the Egyptian desert at Nag Hammadi of a number of scripts purporting to be new "Gospels" (including that of St Thomas which headed up the previous chapter) and other works, including excerpts from the *Corpus Hermeticum*—the ancient Egyptian tradition. These documents were written in the ancient Egyptian language of Coptic, and are Gnostic treatises. So for the first time, a positive and unbiased account of Gnostic literature became available, from which modern-day scholars have pieced together a substantial account of what the Gnostics were about. So what actually were they about?

The Gnostic Myth

The Gnostics used myth as a means of conveying their principles and belief systems. As is normal for myths, not least those in the Bible, such as Adam and Eve, and the myths and fables of ancient Greece, they sound faintly ridiculous to the Western ear, familiar as that is with literal interpretations and unfamiliar with allegory. Going back to not either/or but both/and, we need the intuitive and right-brained approach to work in sympathy with the reasoned and left-brained approach if we are to make any sense out of these tales. Let's take a look at the Gnostic myth of creation and human evolution.

The Gnostic idea of God is a single, non-dual, spiritual essence. He or she is known as the Monad, a term familiar in Plato and the ancient Greek tradition, who finds his way into much Gnostic literature. The Monad is hermaphroditic, and is not capable of being defined other than negatively—one can say what he or she is not, but no positive pronouncement can be made. Only by merging in the Monad can there be any true comprehension. The Monad is said to dwell in the pleroma. The pleroma means "fullness and light". It contains the aeons, who are emanations of aspects of the Divine, which, in pairs, disseminate the Divine light throughout the creation, descending via the lower material areas, and ultimately returning to the One via Gnosis.

The lowest of the aeons is Sophia—wisdom. She apparently had desires and curiosities, and wanted to know the Monad directly. But she was not able to attain that height. She fell from grace, below the level of the pleroma, and engaged with nothingness. The result of this union was a child born of ignorance. This child was called Ialdabaoth, or Jahweh, or Satan. He knew nothing of the pleroma or the real spiritual existence. He is known as the

Demiurge—another Platonic term. He created the material creation, so is referred to as the creator God. But he is not the real God. This is why he is described in Exodus as the "jealous God". He is portrayed as something of a monster and some Gnostic traditions hold him as the personification of evil, and therefore that matter, his creation, is thereby evil by association. This creation was administered by archons. The Demiurge in Plato is not so negatively portrayed, where he is referred to as the craftsman or builder. The Valentinian Gnostics (probably the most substantial Gnostic sect) took a similar view.

The problem for the Demiurge, however, was that he was unable to complete his creation. Something with life or consciousness was needed, and that was only available with the help of his mother, Sophia. It was through her influence that every sentient being was endowed with a spiritual essence. Importantly, it was by this means that a part of the Monad, or "Divine spark" is thus contained within the fabric of each human being and all created beings. This is another link with the Vedanta ("all that lives is full of the Lord"—the opening words of the Isha Upanishad).

This Divine spark is fanned from time to time by avatars, or teachers such as Jesus Christ. Their ministrations provide the means whereby we humans can have direct experience, or knowledge of the Divine—Gnosis. In that way, the journey back to the pleroma can be enacted. To embark upon this journey, however, implies a certain amount of evolution, and the Gnostic teaching recognises three divisions of humanity. The lowest is the body-centred, or hylic (from the Greek *hyle*, or "matter"). The second is the soul/mind-centred, or psychic, sometimes called n*ous*. The third is spirit-centred, or pneumatic. The body is the creation of the Demiurge, whose minions, the archons, are responsible for the evil and negative tendencies. The hylic is essentially animalistic and bound by the appetites and sensations of the body.

The influence of the archons even pervert the dissemination of the teachings of the avatars, thus contaminating truths and words of wisdom into hard doctrinal "religions" that hold back humankind, rather than uplifting humanity. So the psychics are in an intermediate position, partially influenced by the archons, and operating in the world comprising our emotional and mental states, including our ego or persona (little I). But the Divine spark is available in us all, and this transcends the "soul" state. This emanates from the pleroma, and is exemplified in the "pneumatic" person. Gnosis is the means whereby the soul/mind is united with the spirit—the myth of the mystical wedding.

The soul is not the Self, as it stands at a midpoint between the animalistic and the Divine. This is something that is found in many other non-dual traditions, including Mahayana Buddhism and Advaita Vedanta. The whole point is the return of the soul to the source, and for unity to be experienced. The soul is that which is in need of redemption—the body is very temporary and disintegrates upon death, and the spirit is by definition perfect anyway. So the soul needs to be perfected to the extent that he or she is in a fit state to be wedded to the "bridegroom"(referred to as a prince in Gnostic mythology).

The implications for us are that if our soul is wedded to animal passions only, then we will make no progress and will remain base and course. We become our own mini-demiurges, characterised by ignorance and arrogance. But with guidance, there is an optimistic future because darkness cannot survive when light is availed. So once the soul perceives the spirituality of its future, it becomes apparent to it that the self is Divine. It is the Source of and for all. So it is universal and non-dual in its composition. This is the true and inevitable process of Gnosis.

This process implies evolution of the soul—the ascent of the soul by planetary and astrological influences or layers which it needs to transcend. And so, ultimately, the human is fully realised—known as the *andropos*, radiating Divine qualities and residing in the pleroma in a unitive state. The most important point about all this is that because of this potential, all human beings, despite being fallen beings created out of the machinations of the Demiurge, share a Divine essence with the aeons, and so with the Monad. The Gnostic message is therefore fundamentally unitive and positive.

The idea of the reincarnation of the soul is implied in this process. Reincarnation seems to have been accepted at least in some Gnostic traditions, and is referred to by Basilides, a Gnostic teacher, and earlier by Plutarch. The idea was to successively reincarnate the soul until such time that a spiritual direction was accepted, and Gnosis to lead ultimately to realisation, or andropos status. This is spelled out in some of the Nag Hammadi scrolls, notably the "Secret Book of John" which outlines an ongoing process for the soul to purify, ultimately attain Gnosis and so not require further physical embodiment. These teachings can also be found in what is now called Paganism. (There are a number of mystical traditions involving an incarnation of the Divine, including Mithraism, Attis, and perhaps most importantly from Dionysius and Osiris from Egypt. These seemed to be either assimilated into Gnosticism or else eradicated under the strictures of Roman Christianity, in the process of which many of their teachings, calendars, and values were simply regurgitated with a Christian timbre.) In addition, it illustrates a further overlap with Eastern teaching, either Buddhism or the Vedas from India.

Under the Gnostic teaching, there never was a prior "golden age" as outlined in the biblical garden of Eden. So, there was no need for faith to re - access it. There was a fall, but it was of Sophia, wisdom, not of man. Therefore, the harsh doctrine of original sin which afflicts the Judaeo/Christian tradition does not appear in the Gnostic. If faith is not required, then knowledge of the Divine (Gnosis) is what is needed to raise humankind from its slumbers and illuminate its ignorance. In this way, the "golden age" is ongoing and permanent, for it comprises the pleroma, to which in the last resort all human beings, insofar as they are identified as *big I*, or the Divine essence, will return. In this way, the Gnostic belief was by way of the transcending of the lower mortal or personal self (known as the eidolon) by way of the "mysteries", a process of teaching and refinement which in due course led to the establishment in the being of the true divine Self, the daemon. The tale of the goddess Sophia, falling from her celestial abode and abused and ignored by humanity, thus illustrates human potential for realisation when one understands that it is only through true wisdom that the fallen being can be led back to his or her true abode of unity and peace.

The reason for the angst felt by the established church is now clear to see. The ultimate fulfilment of human evolution does not depend upon clearance of original sin. The Gnostic view is that the Divine is within us all and is not just the prerogative of the chosen few, a chosen religious way or a chosen belief system. It is not a question of the duality of me here and God there. With reincarnation, there is an ongoing process to allow the human to evolve, learn, and purify.

The flexible, mystical and tolerant approach of Gnosticism must have been anathema to those taking a dogmatic, doctrinal, and literalist view of the teachings of Christ in the manner apparently ordained under the rule of Constantine in the fourth century CE and his advisors. In such circumstances there was plainly no need for the sale of "forgivenesses". There is no requirement for a privileged group of clerics whom we must engage in order to make any progress. Under Gnosticism women were treated equally to men. Jesus may or may not have been a physical being—what is far more important from the Gnostic perspective is the fact that he was a great teacher and expounder of truth, required to rescue us from materialism and doctrinal control. There may or may not have been a trial and crucifixion (some Gnostic teachings suggest that the crucifixion is an allegory—it is the ego or persona which is crucified, enabling the true self to rise and ascend into heaven—pleroma). Indeed, tales involving being raised from the dead, like Lazarus, were considered allegories of being elevated from being liberated from the throes of bondage to the lower mortal self and inhabiting instead the unitive state of the higher self.

This combination of ideas was totally unacceptable to the early Roman church, which branded such believers as heretics, as this far more inclusive version of the Christian teachings posed an obvious threat to what became the established church. This ultimately resulted in the full power of the Roman establishment wheeled into play, resulting in turn of a cruel and brutal suppression of the Gnostic way, which had to be content with little support until 1945, at which stage the real position became available for study and perusal by scholars such as Elaine Pagels (American scholar and researcher who appraised the Nag Hammadi library and examined and outlined the profound implications thereof), and latterly Freke and Gandy,[3] Tobias Churton, and Andrew Phillip Smith,[4] all of whom have contributed with some wonderfully illuminating books from which the study of what is here called mindful philosophy can be undertaken.

The Ongoing Gnostic Tradition

Gnosticism is held by many scholars to exemplify duality, because it starts from the premise that matter is intrinsically evil and spirituality is intrinsically good. This appraisal misconstrues the essence of the teaching, which is based on the reunification of the divinity in man with the Divine essence, using higher knowledge, or Gnosis, as the key. There cannot be two Divine essences. And Gnosis itself is described as a unitive state. If it is the single non-dual Divine essence to which we all return, then how can there be any separation between us? Truly, when seen from this perspective, Gnosticism is non-dual. The duality is only in relation to the "passing show" and not ultimate reality.

In the Gospel of St John, we find the words "I and my father are one", succinctly encapsulating the unitive Gnostic position. St John and, importantly, St Paul, are two biblical authors whose output has been thoroughly researched with new insights following the release of the Nag Hammadi scrolls by various scholars. Freke and Gandy have made a compelling and thorough case indicating that both were Gnostics. For further information, I can thoroughly recommend their book entitled *The Jesus Mysteries*.

Gnosticism had to endure the verbal onslaught of detractors trying to establish the early church, such as Turtillian and Iraneus, despite receiving apparent approval from others such as Origen and Clement of Alexandria. Some scholars (notably Freke/Gandy in their book *The Jesus Mysteries*) draw parallels of Gnostic teaching with the so-called pagan teaching referred to above, pointing out that we now have an utterly distorted view of these great mystical traditions. Indeed, there is the view that under the pagan umbrella one should include the Greek tradition, including Epictetus, Socrates, Pythagoras, and Aristotle. And Gnosticism as was articulated in the Nag Hammadi writings is a straight derivative of this wondrous background.

Traditions ebb and flow, and ideas come and go, often for no apparent reason, and inexplicably. The Gnostic season seemed to have vanished like snow before the sun. But no matter how thoroughly the Gnostic legacy was trashed, it is just not possible to destroy an idea. The Gnostic idea did survive. It spawned a number of European gatherings, including the Bogomils from Bulgaria and the Cathars. Gnostic ideas inspired some of the great teachers of Europe, including Carl Jung, Rudolph Steiner, and, from earlier years, William Blake, who was a mystic, and the highly influential seventeenth-century German teacher Jacob Bohme, with his notion of the undefinable essence known as the "Ungrund". He inspired the English teacher, William Law, as well as Blake.

Jung is one of the most influential teachers today, and the world of psychotherapy could not have evolved without his teaching, based on an idea of a universal and unformulated "collective unconscious" (pleroma) from which various "archetypes" (aeons) emanated. Individually, these are housed in a "personal unconscious" where they can languish unaccepted by the individual, who uses his ego to reveal what he wishes to. The rest remains as "shadow". The ego is shut away and separated from reality, and it is with the help of the spiritual guide or therapist that appropriate help can be given to illuminate the shadowland—or start the return journey to wholeness or unity. These ideas seem to have a very Gnostic feel, and Jung was a Gnostic himself.

Rudolph Steiner was another luminary who embraced Gnostic ideas. His works span many areas of human activity, drawn up under the banner of "anthroposophy", and deriving material from the Rosicrucians, who also may have used Gnostic teachings. He taught the spiritualisation of creation—the immanent Divine is contained in everything from rocks, through the plant kingdom, vegetation, the animal world, and so to humanity, and beyond. Ultimately, everything is refined and will merge and unite with the source. He saw the make-up of the human being in much the same way as is outlined in the Vedas, with various "bodies" interpenetrating each other, and outlined the need to turn away from materialism. One of his contemporaries, Nicolas Berdyaev, is quoted in the book by A. P. Shepherd on Steiner and his philosophy, *A Scientist of the Invisible*, thus, "Thou art towards a new spirituality and a new mysticism. The new mysticism will not consider this objectivised world as final reality ... In it will be revealed a true gnosis ... And all the tormenting contradictions and divisions will be resolved in the new mysticism, which will be deeper than religions and ought to unite them."[5]

To finish with, let us use a quotation from that great teacher St Paul, whose teachings were unitive in approach and probably derived from Gnosticism according to recent painstaking analysis:

> *Finally brethren, whatsoever things are true, whatsoever things are honest, whatsoever things are just, whatsoever things are pure, whatsoever things are lovely, whatsoever things are of good report, if there be any praise, think on these things. (Philippians 4:8, New English Bible)*

By "think on these things", Paul is inviting us to reflect on them, to let them seep into our values so that they can be realised, and so help humanity return to its true source and unitive state. In the last resort by doing so we can but realise the truth of who we are—the "self-knowledge" proclaimed at Delphi. The ancient pagan and Gnostic "mysteries" are here to show us that what and who we truly are is not the personal, ego embodied self, the eidolon, always becoming but never being, but the daemon, the spiritual essence and the true Self, we have called *big I*.

Viewed from the limitations of the eidolon the daemon is perceived as a separate but spiritually well-disposed adjunct. This is sometimes noted as one's "guardian angel"—a spiritual guide or life coach. But under realisation, "Gnosis", or unity, the so-called guardian angel is seen truly and clearly as being not only what we are, but so is everyone else, and indeed all beings. As such, our spiritual essence inhabits the whole of creation as part of the Divine. "I am thou and thou art I"—this is an ancient pagan and Gnostic statement from the Gnostic treatise "Pistis Sophia" (which means faith in wisdom), then re-materialising in the Gospel of St John as "I in thou and thou in me". And all of this is not so very far from the great Vedic statement "That thou art" or "Thou art That".

Hermeticism

Hermeticism is a term referring to the study of scriptures which taken together comprise the Corpus Hermeticum. They consist of a number of short "books", detailing conversations between one Poimandres, representing the andropos, or quintessential perfect man, who descended to enable matter to be created, and Hermes Trismegistus. Hermes is a Greek name representing the Greek God, and Trismegistus means "thrice great"—great in the gross, subtle, and spiritual worlds. Although Greek terms are used, the thinking is that Hermes actually represents an Egyptian sage as old as, or older than, Moses. He is equated with the Egyptian god Thoth.

The teachings are with reference, once again, to the attainment of Gnosis. The translator's forward in the book *The Way of Hermes*, which is a recent reappraisal of the original writings, contains the following: "The heart of Hermetic teaching … is the realisation that the individual is fundamentally no different from the Supreme."[6] This realisation is what is termed *Gnosis*. This is a path not to be undertaken by standard mental appraisal of the material (i.e., left-brained in modern parlance), but by listening and observing the effect they have on the heart (i.e., intuitive, or right-brained).

It is most interesting to note that within the earthen jar at Nag Hammadi in 1945 were contained not only the Gnostic gospels, but also, in Coptic, a significant part of the Corpus Hermeticum. Quite obviously, the Hermetic data was of major importance to that tradition. From this we can see the thread of non-duality running from the Veda of India, through the ancient Egyptian civilisation, the Gnostics, and with input contemporaneously and later by way of Socrates and the Neoplatonic teachings, then via Ficino through the Florentine renaissance to the present day.

The Hermetic teachings use the term *nous* to describe what one might call higher, or Divine-inspired, mind. The semantics are capable of a number of interpretations, those emanating from the Gnostic tradition using the word *mind* to describe *nous*, and relating the ultimate goal of the perfected being to Gnosis. The "Way of Hermes" leaves the word *nous* untranslated, and avoids reference to the term *Gnosis*, using "knowledge" instead. This matters little—it is quite clear that either way it is through exercising right discrimination that the human soul will either go towards spirituality and will take a higher calibre embodiment if it does so, or will veer towards carnal and bestiality if it does not.

Here is a quotation from book 10 (Way of Hermes version): "The human soul, that is not every human soul, is spiritual and divine. When such a soul has freed itself from the body and passed the test of piety, which is to know God and to harm no man, it becomes pure *nous*. But the impious soul remains in its own substance, restricted by itself, seeking an earthly body, that is to say a human body into which it may enter."

So, reincarnation is the methodology by which we are given the chance of purification and evolution. Towards what? And where? Well, the term *Supreme Good* is used, in Platonic fashion. If right judgement is exercised, then "the soul can pass to a better state, not to a worse. There is a communion of souls and those of the Gods communicate with those of men, those of men with creatures. The stronger take care of the weaker, gods of men and men of creatures and God of all; and all are weaker than him."

The "One" governs via *nous,* said to emanate from the Supreme Good and to be available to all souls, and without which the soul is powerless. Suitably thus equipped, a man is said to be "a divine being and is not to be counted amongst the other creatures on earth but amongst those in heaven called Gods. Indeed, if we have to speak the truth boldly, the true man is above the Gods, or at least fully their equal in power." The golden thread of ultimate unity or non-duality is thus exemplified again.

Turning now to what remains on the ground of this wonderful tradition, it occurred to me that there is a statement in statuesque form in Egypt for all to see. The present archaeological remains of ancient Egypt are remarkably well preserved. Huge, seated monolithic statues can be seen outside the Valley of the Kings, and at Carnac. To my mind, these statues of Rameses and other Egyptian dignitaries owe their imposing presence to the fact that they are sitting in meditation. The back is straight, the head erect, a level gaze, and there is no suggestion of a slouching bodily demeanour. Their pose, no matter what the historical background (often pretty bloodthirsty) is indicative of a culture which was concerned primarily to extol the virtues of Divine union, Gnosis, higher knowledge, call it what you will.

So we now have definitive scripture from the time of Moses or before, and historic artefacts on the ground, which testify to the likelihood of the predominance of a society honouring and living in truth and Divine values.

Sufism

The sun, which is spirit, became separated into rays by the windows, which are bodies. When you gaze on the sun's disk, it

is one, but whoever is screened by his perception of bodies is in
some doubt. Plurality is in the animal spirit; the human spirit
is one essence. Inasmuch as The Divine sprinkled His light upon
humanity, human beings are essentially one. In reality, His light
is never separated.

Jalal al-Rumi[7]

Masnavi II: 186-9

The quote above synthesizes the unity of approach between the Gnostic outlook in which it is demonstrated that each and every being is enlivened by something of the Divine within, and the Hermetic tradition likewise. The Sufi teaching is said to comprise the mystical side of Islam. There are other sources, such as the more recent teacher Idries Shah, which suggest the Sufi way originates much earlier than that, but that it integrated with the Islam tradition in the tenth/eleventh century CE, notably via two masters or *shaikhs*, al-Jilani and as-Suhrawardi, under whose direction it would seem that teaching from both Socrates and the Hermeticum were found to amplify and illustrate the teachings of the Prophet Muhammad. So the Socratic tradition finds its way into both the Christian and Islamic traditions—not something that is held in high profile under the more strident utterances in either.

Sufism is very much "on message" with mindful philosophy because, as amply illuminated by the quote from Rumi above, it embraces the fact that knowledge of the Divine, true knowledge, or ultimate reality (known as *haqiqa)* is available to all. There are necessary qualifications to be in receipt of such knowledge—it is not to be obtained by intellectual, psychological, or physical methodology, but by receiving and reflecting upon and thereupon enacting guidance from a master. In this way, it embarks upon a course akin to that espoused in Advaita Vedanta, which we will consider in chapter six. The idea is not to go down the road of habitual reactions, but to select a lifestyle embracing tranquillity, reflection, and sensory abstinence.

The route to this knowledge is through the process of *dhikr.* Dhikr means awareness of Allah, or the Divine, so is inclusive of any process or activity conducive to that goal. So it might include meditation or spiritual reflection. Also included would be poetry, fine literature, chanting, and dance. The Mevlevi dancing is associated with this tradition, designed to attain the Divine space by complete surrender of egoic tendencies (*nafs)* by way of the association of music and movement (as exemplified by the Whirling Dervishes).

One of the early Sufi teachers, Ibn al-Arabi, expressed the desire of the Sufis to live in a universal world. He taught that the created world is the Divine essence made manifest—something that would be familiar to the Indian Vedantist, as well as the Christian by way of the world being made in the image of God. His approach can be summed up as "love is the faith

I hold, and wheresoever one's camels turn, the one true faith is there". This universal outlook is beautifully expressed similarly as follows: "On my way to the mosque, Oh Lord, I passed the Magian in front of his flame, deep in thought, and a little further I heard a rabbi reciting his holy book in the synagogue. Then I came across the church where the hymns sung gently in my ears, and finally I came into the mosque and pondered how many are the different ways to You—the one God."

The approach illustrated here by Arabi exemplifies a unitive strand of teaching permeating Islam generally, and the mystical Sufi path specifically. Despite the loud protestations of some Islam sects, the fact remains that that tradition has always embraced a degree of universality. The Quran exhibits manifold references to spiritual guides preceding Muhammed, including not only Jesus, for whom there is the highest regard, but also old testament prophets such as Abraham and Moses.

One of the great teachers in the tenth century is Al-Farabi, who advises that truth or wisdom is not the exclusive province of religion, but lies also within the province of philosophy. His approach would have appealed to thinkers today, as it is analytical and scientific, described as a "science of reality". He considered that there was similar validity in the great religious traditions generally, but that the single unitive truth underpinning all of them was capable of a variety of "imaginative representations". Ultimately his view is that philosophically speaking, all the revealed spiritual outlets utter the same guidance in terms of the single substratum and unitive source, because all peoples need to rely upon one and only one explanation of reality. Either that explanation is true or it is not—truth is, by its very nature, unitive, no matter how many and varied might be the manner of its illustration and exposition.

Under Sufi teaching the human being is likely to manifest under one of three influences—*nafs* (lower self, ego, in which case the end result could very probably be a tyrant), *qualb* (heart, likely to manifest in a faith-driven manifestation), and *ruh* (spiritual way). Dhikr, under proper guidance, is what helps the aspirant raise his or her sights from the mundane to the spiritual. There is reference to the "spirit of guidance", meaning the Divine essence, equating to the inner light, Buddha nature, or God within. This is a universal concept, which has here been referred to as *big I*. Some Sufi traditions looked beyond the world of Islam for guidance as to realisation of the spiritual essence, notably Inayatkhan by way of what is known as the Sufi Order of the West.

This can be contentious in the world of Islam, but what is plain to behold is the wholly unambiguous poetry and prose of perhaps the most well-known Sufi sage (at least in the Western world), Rumi. His principle message is that by abandoning the ego (nafs) one can commit to the spiritual essence or Divine (ruh) via truthful living. His output was prodigious and wholly inspiring, helping not only to place the spiritual traditions of Islam in their rightful place within the available knowledge today, but also to educate us in the most succinct way possible as to the veracity of non-dual or universal and inclusive philosophy. Rather like Shakespeare in his sonnets, there is often reference to the beloved or loved one, so that the meaning can either be taken literally or allegorically to mean the spiritual essence. How about this as a peon of praise and rapture of the spirit of non-duality, from his *Divan-e Shams?*

> *I am not of the East, nor of the West, nor of the land, nor of the sea; I am not of Nature's mint, nor of the circling heavens.*
>
> *I am not of the earth, nor of water, nor of air, nor of fire; I am not of the empyrean, nor of dust, nor of existence, nor of entity.*
>
> *I am not of India, nor of China, nor of Bulgaria, nor of Saqsin; I am not of the kingdom of Iraqan, nor the country of Khorasan.*
>
> *I am not of this world, nor of the next, nor of paradise, nor of hell; I am not of Adam, nor of Eve, nor of Eden, nor of Rizwan.*
>
> *My place is the Placeless, my trace is the Traceless; Tis neither body nor soul, for I belong to the soul of the Beloved.*
>
> *I have put duality away, I have seen that the two worlds are one; One I seek, One I know, One I see, One I call. (tr. R.A. Nicholson).*

CHAPTER 5

NON-DUALITY IN THE FAR EASTERN TRADITIONS

One Nature, perfect and pervading, circulates in all natures, One Reality, all comprehensive, contains within itself all realities. The one Moon reflects itself wherever there is a sheet of water, And all the moons in the waters are embraced within the one moon. The Dharma—body (i.e. the Supreme Being) of all the Buddhas enters into my own being. And my own being is found in union with theirs. The Inner Light is beyond praise and blame; Like space it knows no boundaries, Yet it is even here, within us, ever retaining its serenity and fullness.

Yung-chia Ta-shih

Non-duality, as both a spiritual practice and a mode of living, is perhaps more visible and culturally integrated in the East than it is in the West and elsewhere. Specifically, there are two major areas which, for the purposes of exploring non-duality and mindful philosophy, I would like to discuss— Advaita Vedanta from India which forms the subject of the next chapter, and Buddhism, which together with Taoism is the subject now. Buddhism emanated in India from the same stable as the Indian Vedic teachings, relying upon the ancient Upanishads, and in that area retains much of the same nomenclature and terminology (even if it uses the Pali canon to do so, rather than the older Sanskrit tongue of India).

The spread of the Buddhist culture in eastern and northern directions infused it with different traditions, notably Confucionism and, in particular, Taoism, which gave a particular flavour to various Buddhist teachings, notably Zen and some of what is known as Mahayana Buddhism, from which the quotation above is taken. Mindfulness is associated with Buddhism, and as noted in chapter 1, is a major part of the "middle way" or noble eightfold path designed to lead the aspirant to "nirvana", or complete liberation. Buddhism today is flourishing in the West because of its lack of doctrinal dogmas and its compassionate stance, tolerance, and lack of judgementalism.

To look in more detail at this, we will first consider non-duality in those aspects of the Buddhist way where this has been retained or displayed by way of acknowledgement of the "Buddha within". We will consider the yin and the yang of Taoism. These traditions can be discerned as philosophies as opposed to religion, as in no case do they embrace the idea of a personalised God. There are however differences of emphasis, although I suspect these are more manufactured in the semantics and linguistic inadequacies than is perhaps often represented in the textbooks.

Buddhism

Buddhism is a major world philosophical teaching. As such, and perhaps inevitably, it offers a number of differing interpretations of the Buddha's teaching. He was a teacher of universality and non-duality. At the time of the Buddha's searching for enlightenment there were serious problems with the prevailing Hindu culture, notably corruption within the caste system, thus necessitating a different methodology.

The Buddha achieved "enlightenment" in approximately 528 BCE. He didn't pursue the road of acknowledging a Supreme Being. However, within the Dhammapada, there are a number of illuminating statements, such as when addressing the issue of "self-possession", the Buddha is reported as saying in verse 160: "Only a man himself can be the master of himself: who else from outside can be his master? When the Master and servant are one, then there is true help and self-possession."

Elsewhere there is the following: "Of what use are words of wisdom to the man who is unwise? Of what use is a lamp to a blind man? Hear the essence of thousands of sacred books: to help others is virtue; to hurt others is sin. A man rises or goes down by his own actions ... The narrow-minded man thinks and says: 'This man is one of us; this one is not, he is a stranger. To the man of noble soul the whole of mankind is but one family.'"

So we can easily see the "compassionate Buddha" outlining a pathway for his followers including a refusal to see separation, which is one of the hallmarks of mindful philosophy. The idea is to use the teaching of loving kindness and compassion to transcend the obstacles of *dukkha*, or pain, torment and so on. However, in some quarters, Buddhism is perceived as ultimately no more than nihilism. Nirvana is said to comprise nothing but a void. In the last resort, there is nothing.

This to my mind is an erroneously negative interpretation of the teachings. Because there was no endeavour to subscribe to the notion of a Supreme Being does not invalidate the teaching of *Dharma* (meaning, "the law", ethical code of conduct, and so on—this is featured in the Advaita Vedanta way equally) or the four noble truths, or the eightfold path. It ultimately comes down to the fact that true unity with the Divine (or whatever one calls it) goes beyond the capacity of language, which fails at that stage. It is simply not competent to relay that which cannot be described. So one can do no more than either use the nomenclature of the Brihadaranyaka Upanishad we have already seen (the ultimate is "not this, not this") or admit defeat and indicate "nothing"—or more precisely, "no thing". The mystic has to resort to notions of nothingness to describe the highest echelons of existence. No words are competent to describe the indescribable, so one cannot call it something. And reason tells us that if Nirvana is the epitome of bliss and universality, how can this be known to be so without it having either been witnessed or integrated with?

The Mahayana strain of Buddhism goes further down the road of spirituality as a universal concept, by virtue of its embracement of the idea of something of the Buddha deeply embedded in humanity—the "Buddha within". So the Buddha is an incarnation of what is known by the Mahayanists as *Dharmakaya*, or "suchness", which can be loosely translated as the Absolute, also described above as the "Buddha within". The Buddha within, or one's "Buddha nature" is the ultimate changeless reality, ultimately all that can be said to exist, and an entity which is not accessible via the ordinary conceptualising mind.

The approach required to receive any kind of comprehension is intuitive, and will not manifest if there is any notion in the aspirant of wanting or getting a result. This, in turn, requires the mind to be at rest so that the innumerable thoughts, desires, fears, and opinions which so intrude upon the consciousness can be laid to rest. So to enter this state of being, meditation is the key. Otherwise, the world, known as *samsara*, although illusory, assumes an apparent reality and permanence, and the aspirant is bound in the state of worldliness, which cannot compare with the all-embracing, unmanifested, but ultimately wholly real Buddha nature, the integration with which ultimately constitutes nirvana.

Another feature of the Mahayana teaching was that despite the denial or refusal (because of the particular monastic circumstances the Buddha was creating) to countenance the idea of Self or atman, the Buddhist way evolved around a non-personal entity, devoid of any conscious notion of a Divine entity. In this manner, the creators of some of the sutras, no doubt due to direct spiritual experience, refer to the idea of "universal mind". Universal mind for these purposes can be equated with big I, or pure consciousness. This is something to which the suitably purified and refined individual mind will ultimately integrate, this being the ultimate goal of the Buddhist aspirant. Here is a quotation from an early Zen teaching from the Lankavatara Sutra in which it is being explained that the Buddhist aspirant requires the intuitive spiritual approach as well as reason:

> *Those who vainly reason without understanding the truth are lost in the jungle of the Vijnanas (lower knowledge, the world), running about here and there and trying to justify their view of ego substance. The Self realised in your inmost consciousness appears in its purity; this is the "Tathagata—garbha" (Buddha nature, Universal Mind), which is not the realm given of those given over to mere reasoning. Pure in its own nature, free from the category of the finite and infinite, Universal Mind is the undefiled "Buddha womb", which is wrongly apprehended by sentient beings.*

This doesn't sound like a nihilist approach to me.

Mahayana Buddhism also espouses the notion of a threefold manifestation of the "threefold bodies" of the Buddha. These comprise the material body (*nirmanakaya*) in which the universal mind is incarnated within a human being as an actual teacher or avatar, the creator or personal "God" or

Divine entity (*sambhogakaya*) and the "clear light of the void", the ultimate primordial Buddha (*Dharmakaya*). This trinity of metaphysical entities does carry strong resonance with similar situations in the Christian and Hindu teachings.

The ancient teaching of Taoism is associated with China, and had a very significant influence on certain strands of Mahayana Buddhism, to the extent that there is a very similar "sound" to both these teachings. The Taoist school had espoused a non-dualistic and holistic approach, which predated the arrival of the Buddhist culture. A specific appraisal of Taoism is featured later, but to illustrate the essential unity between Taoism and Mahayana Buddhism here is a sample of Taoist teaching:

> *Empty yourself of everything. Let the mind rest in peace. The ten thousand things rise and fall, while the Self watches their return. They grow and flourish, and then return to the Source. Returning to the Source is stillness, which is the way of nature. Knowing constancy is insight. Not knowing constancy leads to disaster. Knowing constancy the mind is open. With an open mind you will be open hearted. Being open hearted you will act royally. Being royal, you will attain the Divine. Being Divine, you will be at One with the Tao. Being at One with the Tao is eternal. And although the body dies, the Tao will never pass away.*
>
> *Tao Te Ching, ch. 16*

This is a powerful piece of spiritual advice which informed the emergence of what we call Zen Buddhism, which was a school of Mahayana Buddhism. Under Taoist influence, this school developed throughout China and the Far East, Japan, and Korea. *Zen* is a corruption of the Chinese word *chan*, meaning meditation. *Chan* is the Japanese pronunciation of that word (*dzjen*), and ultimately comes from the Sanskrit word for meditation, *dhyana*. Mindfulness practice is required in order to be aware of the breath, and of the various energy centres in the body. This also assists in observing the mind, simply witnessing thoughts as they rise and fall, and withdrawing attention from them.

This is a major area where Zen is at one with the other main wisdom traditions, including Advaita, Socrates, and Gnosticism, so that by exercising mind control the being simply negates all ideas of "doing" and retains a deep stillness or awareness. Thus, the essence of the Zen teaching is meditation (*zazen*), to accompany the highest standards of personal behaviour and lifestyle, and thus realising one's Buddha nature. Having realised this, it can be practiced in the life and taken out into the world for the benefit not of oneself, but others—the universal as opposed to the individual. A guide or teacher is needed in order to comprehend the koans, teachings and sutras from spiritual texts, and to implement the *dhamma*, or "law, ethical code of conduct". The outcome of this process of refinement, which takes place after as many lifetimes as is necessary, is merging in nirvana. Some fully realised beings continue to assist humankind (bodhisattvas).

The Zen/Mahayana/Taoist teachings are of the utmost importance in our endeavours to appreciate mindful or non-dual philosophy as the golden thread referred to earlier running throughout human spirituality. It will have become apparent by now that we aren't trying to identify a "master teaching" or "master religion". We are identifying the common factor uniting all great teaching. Spiritual leaders were just that—the religions and doctrinal schools of thought came later. I do not think there is any spiritual teaching which has not to greater or lesser extent suffered from its over enthusiastic devotees who tend to misconstrue the universalistic approach that the greatest teachers reveal, then endeavour to, as it were, ring-fence or cherry-pick their favourite pieces, then codify or dogmatise them, and so sow the seeds of dissention and exclusivity at the expense of unity and inclusivity. The Buddha expressly stated that he was not a god. Nor did he claim to be an angel or a spirit. What he did say was that he was *awake*.

Awake! What really does that mean? After all, I am thinking I'm awake as I write this. And I guess you are thinking likewise as you read these words. But are we? And what is the Buddha trying to tell us?

Mindful philosophic teaching, including as it does the essence of the Advaita and Mahayana schools, recognises that there are various levels of awareness. I will be devoting space later to consider these in detail, but for now I can summarise these briefly as follows:

There is deep sleep. That much is familiar. All one has to do is to rest and receive the sleep. In that state, there is not a lot of awareness or consciousness—although there is a little. Mothers can be aware of the well-being of their babies even under the state of deep sleep. Then there is the dream state—sweet dreams or nightmares. Both, however, seem illusory when one emerges into what we call the "real world". Now, what happens then? There seems to be a choice. Either we can adopt a mechanistic, habit-driven path, or we can indeed be "fully awake" and retain full awareness. The former approach can be said to equate to "waking sleep". It is the opposite of being fully awake.

How many times have we got up, attended to one's ablutions, breakfasted, journeyed to work or the shops, performed one's tasks, and so on, without really having "been there" at all? It is as if we are in autopilot mode. The wonders of creation, the people who we meet, the world and everything in it simply pass us by. This is something we will be considering more deeply in the chapter on mindful practice, but for the moment, let us simply acknowledge that as far as the Buddhist advice is concerned, we do not have to live our lives like automatons, railroaded from one uninspiring situation to the next. We can be fully awake, with all senses and attributes fully attuned. More of this anon, but before leaving this discussion, we might take guidance from the mystics, who advise that there is a state even beyond that—the state (if such it be) of unity, of full unitive awareness, of Divine realisation, *samadhi*, self-realisation, or whatever. That is what being really *awake* means. And that is not just for the favoured few—it is the birthright and ultimate destiny of us all.

In the Mahayana Buddhist tradition, as is the case in all areas where philosophy is expounded and enacted mindfully, there is a requirement for the aspirant, en route to realisation of the Buddha within, to allow that to take place not so much by doing things as by simply allowing that state of being to reveal itself by eschewing any idea of ego or individual persona centredness, whether in the discursive mind by way of desires or fears, the intellect, the imagination, or in the will. This is the essence of the four noble truths, and is expounded in various sutras, one of which is known in translation as "the awakening of faith" by the Indian sage Ashvaghosha. The original Sanskrit version is lost, but under the Chinese translation it outlines a number of "expedient means" by which unity can be availed. Two of these are helpful in a consideration of non-duality: the way of tranquillity and the way of wisdom.

As far as the way of tranquillity is concerned, the idea is to allow the thoughts and emotions in the mind to come to rest, and so allow them to be observed, and so appraised. This is a twofold process known as "stopping and realising" and so allowing simple observation to predominate. This can include the various thought processes and emotions but not to the extent that they are allowed to take over the attention. The idea is to consciously let them pass. This is known as "right mentation" so that any trace of the individual ego self is transcended as one adopts the fact of the existence of one's true essence. This process allows insight to become established, and so able to embark upon the second area—the way of wisdom. This is where mindfulness comes in.

Whatever befalls the individual, whether walking, talking, feeling, breathing, eating, abluting, or whatever, is simply placed under dispassionate non-judgemental observation. No comment is necessary. So—it's not about "I am breathing, and I feel good about that. Now I am walking, and I'm finding it boring. Now I am eating and am finding this agreeable and so on". It is rather "There is breathing. There is walking. There is boredom", and so on. One just lets the attention rest upon what is in front of one without comment, and so stays detached and uninvolved. This will produce steadiness of being, and with diligent practice, real tranquillity. There is freedom from the tyranny of the mind and the power of the senses, also freedom from the domination over the being of greed, anger, lust, pride, infatuation, and in short, all potentially undesirable aspects of the ego, or small self—"little I". This is a "big ask" for most of us. Help and direction will be needed. But the prize is equanimity of being, peace, a compassionate and loving disposition, and no suggestion whatsoever of dualism.

Taoism and the Taijitu Symbol

Before we leave the non-dual offerings of the far East, there is one further interesting demonstration of non-duality which we could consider. We have already referred to the ancient Chinese tradition of Taoism. This teaching has given us a beautifully succinct methodology of comprehending unity. It is known as the *taijitu* symbol, as illustrated thus:

DIAGRAM OF TAIJITU SYMBOL

The taijitu diagram is often seen as the illustration of what in Chinese philosophy is known as the yin and the yang. Nature is always endeavouring to procure a balance. This is something not foreign to the Native American tradition, too. Whenever there is an imbalance, forces are awakened to correct it. It is as if there are polarities of influence. To take a simple example, if one travels progressively in a westward direction over the surface of the Earth, which is spherical, one will ultimately emerge in the East. (And of course, *vice versa).* This balancing out is referred to as the yin and the yang. So, when the yang attains its peak, it retreats to allow the yin to evolve likewise. There are pairs of opposites running right through creation. These pairs are what is referred to in the Tao Te Ching quote above as the "ten thousand things". They are many and varied. Here are a few: male/female, bright/dark, tall/short, rich/poor, good/bad, up/down, flexible/rigid, problem/opportunity, true/untrue, good/evil, rich/poor, happiness/misery. One could create endless more.

Now the diagram itself is perfectly balanced. The point is that each implies and ultimately depends upon the other. If we consider the yin and the yang, for example, we can perceive the yin as female, so as intuitive, emotionally driven, complex, receptive, negative, and yielding. By the same token, the yang is perceivable as male, rational, positive, simple, active, creative. The yin is sometimes referred to as the soul, endowed with wisdom (as Sophia in Gnosticism), and yang as the intellect. They plainly need each other. And that is how the system works. After all, how do we know something is short unless there is something tall to compare it with? The diagram includes a particle of the black within the white, and vice versa.

So, within the male, to ensure balance and harmony, there needs to be a piece of the female. It is not a case of *either* male *or* female, but *both* male *and* female. Neither can survive without the other. And this is a perspective that can inform our lifestyle, our day-to-day decision taking and outlook, and can let our deeper nature of inclusivity be nurtured and fully propagated. It has been referred to by many teachers and philosophers, including Darrell Reanney in his book *The Music of the Mind*, and by Timothy Freke in his book *The Mystery Experience*, and by Malcolm Hollick in his book *The Science of Oneness*.[1,2] I would commend all these very different, but ultimately unitive, approaches to the serious mindful philosophy student.

Mindful philosophy teaching adds a new twist to this scenario. The real self (not the false idea of self) is unaffected and identifies with neither of the halves of the pairs outlined in the taijitu symbol. This is a somewhat paradoxical situation which, whilst readily apparent in all-inclusive traditions, is perhaps most easy to perceive in the Advaita Vedanta data, reliant as it is upon the extraordinary, powerful, and wholly loving teachings to be found in the Bhagavad Gita.

So that is where we go next. For the moment, we need to appreciate that the far eastern teachings have offered seekers in the West a beautiful and pure expression of unity, unsullied by repeated interpretations of scriptural authority which has bedevilled so many other pathways. The emphasis on mindfulness and meditation seems to have delivered something of huge value to the Western world. Those seeking to learn from this tradition are probably under the notion that some form of enlightenment is needed.

So let the last word on this noble tradition come from the great Buddhist contemporary teacher, Thich Nhat Hanh, who in his book *Going Home* advises:

> *What is enlightenment? Again, an idea about enlightenment is not enlightenment. Look into yourself, and you know that enlightenment is something you may have within yourself. When you begin to understand, when you have been able to free yourself from a notion, that is enlightenment. And you have been enlightened so many times in the past. You have suffered because of these things and when you got out of these illusions and wrong perceptions, enlightenment was born in you. Don't say that enlightenment is foreign to you. You know what it is. When you drink coffee, when you hold the hand of a child and walk, when you are really there, fully present and concentrated, you enjoy it more. You understand more of what is going on. That is mindfulness. That is concentration. That kind of mindfulness, concentration, and insight improves your happiness, your peace. That is universal.*

CHAPTER 6

ADVAITA VEDANTA

If you begin to be what you are, you will realise everything, but to begin to be what you are, you must first come out of what you are not. You are not those thoughts which are turning, turning in your mind. You are not those changing feelings. You are not the different decisions you make and the different wills you have. You are not that separate ego.

Well then, what are you? You will find that when you have come out of what you are not, that the ripple on the water is whispering to you "I am That", that the birds in the trees are singing to you "I am That", the moon and the stars are shining beacons to you "I am That". You are in everything in the world and everything in the world is reflected in you. And at the same time you are That—everything.

Sri Shantananda Saraswati, Good Company[1]

To know what you are, you must first investigate and know what you are not. And to know what you are not, you must watch yourself carefully, rejecting all that does not necessarily go with the basic fact: "I AM". The ideas: "I am born at a given place, at a given time, from my parents, and now I am so—and—so, living at, married to, father of, employed by", and so on, are not inherent in the sense "I AM". Our usual attitude is of "I am this". Separate consistently and perseveringly the "I am" from "this" or "that" and try to feel what it means to BE, just to BE, without being "this" or "that".

Sri Nisargatta Maharaj, I Am That[2]

Advaita Vedanta—An Introduction

Advaita Vedanta is a teaching which is totally and unambiguously committed to non-duality. As stated, the word *Advaita* is a Sanskrit term meaning literally "not two". It is probably the oldest world teaching. Like all man-made interpretations, it has suffered its ups and downs, including some corruption of its output in the 500-600s BCE, which in turn created the impetus for Buddhism to emerge. It received a reinvigoration about a thousand years later courtesy of a philosopher and saint, Adi Shankara.

As Plato and Socrates could arguably be considered the master philosophical teachers of the Western world, so Shankara could arguably be considered likewise in the case of the East. This is due to his capacity to embrace and articulate the notion of non-duality like no other through his treatises on the Bhagavad Gita, the Upanishads, and a number of original works. His genius was to be able to offer this both in terms of appealing to reason and knowledge (*jnana*), which he did by scrupulously applying line-by-line analysis to some seriously substantial spiritual works, but also appealing to love or devotion (*bhakti*), which he did in an outpouring of beautifully crafted poems of hymns to the universal *Brahman*.

Today, it is clear that non-duality, or Advaita, is another Eastern teaching which is finding favour in the West. There are schools of Advaita teaching across the globe and leading exponents of Advaita have seen the need for spiritual resurgence in the West, because of the apparent foundering of some of the Western indigenous religious or spiritual teachings. This resulted in the availability of *transcendental meditation* in the Western world. Teachers like Ramakrishna and Vivekananda, noted for his visits and lectures in the nineteenth century in the United States and Europe, paved the way for a rich offering of Indian spiritual books and texts on the subject of universality and spiritual inclusivity. Guides such as Mother Meera have established bases in Europe, and the creator of the above quotation, Sri Shantananda Saraswati, and his successor have been receiving Western visitors from a number of organisations and thereby providing hugely important and invaluable guidance of a most practical type for the benefit of the likes of you and me.

And today we have a considerable collection of gurus and teachers who collectively could be described as part of the Neo-Advaita movement, deriving from such luminaries as Nisargadatta Maharaj, who is also quoted above, Ramana Maharshi, Ramakrishna, and Krishnamurti, which we will be looking at later, in chapter 8. Today, we are the fortunate recipients of the leading contemporary exponents of the tradition of Advaita Vedanta, namely via the teaching of the eighth-century philosopher and guide Adi Shankara, continuing today as the teaching of Shankara by way of the Shankaracharya tradition. (*Acharya* is a Sanskrit word meaning "teacher", so *Shankaracharya* means "teacher of the way of Shankara"). These will be considered in the next chapter.

Advaita Vedanta starts by acknowledgement of the single non-dual substratum which is referred to as *Brahman.* There is and can be no definition of the Brahman other than by seeing what it is not. Anything and everything that may be perceptible to the senses (hearing, seeing, touching, tasting, and smelling) and also via the mind cannot be Brahman. The teaching however states that the true self of every human being, or the *atman,* is not separate from, or different from, the universal Brahman. There is also the notion of the supreme self, the *paramatman,* to emphasise the universal nature of the spiritual essence of humankind.

The Philosophy of Advaita Vedanta

The first, most significant and most burning question of any philosopher has to be "what, in truth, am I?" or to put it another way: "What, in truth, is a human being?" Advaita explains that because there can be no separation of the self of the so-called individual from the Divine, that I am divine. Now if one revisits the first paragraph of the beautiful first quotation that heads up this chapter, maybe this will start to make sense. Shantananda Saraswati is starting us off from the notion of "Self-Enquiry" (if you want to be what you are). He then states that the first step is to sever identification from what one is not (so not the physical body, not the thoughts in the mind, nor the emotions and feelings. Not the will, or even what he terms the separate ego or persona.)

Having emerged from all of that, one has to ask—is there anything left? Well, of course, there is. Someone is observing all that is going on. And that something is none other than yourself. The Self is the witness, the observer, the essence who is unattached to the things of creation. The second quotation follows virtually an identical pattern, using the notion "I am" as the ultimate statement of truth. To sum this up, the philosophy of Advaita and of mindful philosophy contains this master statement: "You cannot be anything you can observe."

This can take some getting used to, but just consider. Reason tells us that the subject cannot be the object. If *you* are doing the observing, how could *you* possibly be the simultaneous object of that observation? This is succinctly encapsulated by the well-known modern spiritual teacher Eckhart Tolle in his book *Stillness Speaks* in the following terms: "You say, 'I want to know myself'. You *are* the I. You *are* the knowing. You *are* the consciousness through which everything is known. And that cannot KNOW itself; it IS itself."[3]

The effect of this is profound indeed, because it places human identification not on a gross physical level, not on the level of the machinations of the mind, not on the ever changing world of the emotions, and not on the notion of "little I" or the ego, but fairly and squarely upon big I, the Divine spark or Self, the atman. This atman is not different in all creatures, although it shines through all of us in the way we as individual creatures have evolved. If we can equate Self with consciousness, then it is quite easy to see that one cannot visualise one lot of consciousness in a pot as it were over here, and another lot in another pot over there.

But without consciousness, there is nothing whatsoever. So consciousness can be said to be everywhere and everywhen. As such, it can be said to be *both* immanent *and* transcendent. Immanence and transcendence are two terms that are familiar to the Christian and other traditions. The Self transcends all in creation—that is what is meant by the phrase *not this, not this*. This is something the Buddhists grappled with and decided that language cannot get there, so they resorted to "no thing", or the "void". It is simply not possible to procure any form of pat definition for this, the biggest subject of all.

However, insofar as there is consciousness and awareness to greater or lesser extent in all, it can be said to reside immanent throughout creation.

So the second paragraph of Shantananda Saraswati's quotation ("you will find when you have come out of what you are not, that the ripple on the water, etc. ...") illustrates most movingly how this immanence is experienced. The first paragraph is "not this, not this". In other words, "I" am transcendent in relation to all of this, and the second paragraph sees no separation—total and complete unity (you are in everything in the world, and everything in the world is reflected in you, and at the same time you are that—everything).

Under this tradition, there is reference to the threefold nature of us all that we looked at briefly in chapter 2. At this stage, I think it is well to recap and perhaps look a little more deeply at the implications of these three things, which are universally accepted and common to all human beings. They are the notions of truth, consciousness, and true happiness/bliss. These are known in the ancient Vedic language of Sanskrit as *sat*, *chit*, and *ananda* respectively, and one comes across the composite word *satchitananda* to define the threefold nature of us all. This is something that can quite easily be recognised. For example, when considering truth, it can be easily acknowledged that no one knowingly would *not* want the truth. It is deeply ingrained in all of us that the untruth is unacceptable. We looked at the ideas of truth being not "true for me", or "my truth", because whilst that may indeed be the case for the individual egoic entity we have christened "little I", that way lies a particular belief system, creed, code of conduct. One ultimately might wish to refine, change, or destroy that particular belief system, creed, or code of conduct. It is therefore partial, not universal, so less than absolute. Here is a tale from *Lamps of Fire* by Juan Mascaro to illustrate the point:

> *One day a king called one of his ministers and told him: "Go, good fellow, and bring here all the men of the town that were born blind". When the blind men had all been assembled, the king told a servant: "Show these men an elephant". The servant did as he was commanded, and he made one blind man touch the head of the elephant, another the ear, another the trunk, the tail, and the tuft of the tail. To each he said that he was touching the elephant. After this the king went to the blind men and asked them: "now that you have touched the elephant, tell me your conclusions". The man who had touched the head said: "it is like a pot". The one who touched the ear said: "it is like a fan". And so for the others, the trunk was like a plough, a tusk a plough share, a foot a pillar, the tail a pestle, the back a granary, and the tuft of the tail a broom. And each blind man thought that what he had touched was the elephant. And then they began to argue and to quarrel, stating: "an elephant is like this"—"no, it is like this"—"I tell you it is not"; and so on, until in the end they came to blows.[4]*

The elephant in this tale represents truth. Each blind man appraised the particular part of it correctly. But because his view was only partial, he was not able to see the true and full picture; his view was but partial, and so was his understanding. Under Advaita Vedanta, truth is the bedrock of this teaching, and indeed the bedrock for mindful philosophy if the goal is true knowledge or wisdom, and that is what this story is trying to convey.

The great teachers, such as Socrates, Jesus, or Shankara, advise that truth is the steady state of quiet peace and stillness of mind from which truthfulness arises and is part of. Truth is that which is permanent. So, truth is where you are coming from, not where you are going to. Even would-be wrongdoers need to be able to trust their colleagues in crime. The primary goal of dialectic, according to Socrates, is that truth is the goal.

Secondly, there is the idea of consciousness. We considered this before to the extent that without consciousness, there is no life, nothing. So it is easy to see that consciousness is universal, and when all else is discarded or unavailed, it is just consciousness that is left. Consciousness pervades the whole of creation whether immanent within it, or transcendent outside it. It pervades us, too. Consciousness has been likened to water. In its solid state, water is ice, and has little or no movement. In its liquid form, it manifests as flowing water. In its gaseous form, it manifests as steam, and is diffused in an undifferentiated manner. Likewise, consciousness in its solid state manifests as the physical creation. In its liquid state, it manifests as thoughts and ideas, emotions, and personas. In its final pure form, it permeates and infuses everything in creation in an undifferentiated and formless manner. So consciousness is life and is paramount in the make-up of a human. After all, no matter what our beliefs and background, most of us would readily acknowledge that life must be preserved at all cost.

Lastly, there is bliss, joy, or true happiness. This can sometimes seem a little too good to be true. But reason advises that any human activity is instigated by the desire for happiness. No matter how misguided or ultimately erroneous that result might be, the fact remains that the motivating factor for human decision taking is ultimately a perception that "I" will be the happier if that decision is embarked upon. Advaita philosophy refines this immediately, encouraging this to be viewed from a big or universal stance and not from a tightly controlled world of just "me and mine". But even in this tiny world, the inevitable conclusion is that it is the desire for well-being that fuels our decisions. Under Advaita teaching, one starts from a "reality check"—the acknowledgement that because big I is the true Self, he or she is whole, complete, and free, and so is intrinsically happy and blissful.

The problems start when notions creep into the mind, based upon premises that "I" cannot be happy unless and until certain criteria are met. For example, "I will be happy once my mortgage is paid off", or "when I retire", or "once I've got out of this situation", "when my ship comes in" or "once I've met the partner of my dreams". Well, it is not so. True and lasting happiness and well-being under mindful philosophy teachings as exemplified under Advaita aren't dependent upon a *thing*. The above scenarios all have their equal and opposite situation, resulting in the manifestation of misery or pain. Pleasures and happiness which are dependent will not last—they are ephemeral. True happiness is *Self*-dependent. There is no down side. This is true contentment. Whilst one does not wish to belittle human suffering or lack, the true follower of Advaita sees all this as part of a play—the *maya*, and not ultimately real. I will enlarge upon this theme in the chapter on mindful practice, but for the moment the important point is that through this approach the Advaita aspirant is able to maintain equanimity even in the most appalling human situations.

Truth, consciousness, and bliss, then, are the three component parts of the true self, atman, or big I. Under Advaita teaching, they are said to arise totally naturally if we can make sure that the "not self" is kept out of harm's way, and so does not cover our essential nature. It might be helpful therefore to consider a little more deeply how we recognise just what we are, and so do as recommended and "come out of what we are not". How is this done?

What You Are

The nineteenth-century teacher Swami Vivekananda was renowned across the West as an exponent of Indian thought, particularly in the United States. He was a disciple of the great teacher and saint Ramakrishna, and between them they became the most well-known exponents of Advaita philosophy at the turn of the nineteenth and twentieth centuries. Vivekananda is quoted in the book *Insights into Vedanta* by Swami Sunirmalanda in which he gave a particularly succinct and clear exposition of what *you*, the atman, actually are. Here is an extract:

> *The different philosophies seem to agree that this ATMAN, whatever it be, has neither form nor shape, and that which has neither form nor shape must be omnipresent … Time, space and causation, therefore are in the mind. As this Atman is beyond the mind and is formless, it must be beyond time, beyond space, and beyond causation.*
>
> *Now, if it is beyond time, space, and causation, it must be infinite. Then comes the highest speculation of our philosophy. The infinite cannot be two. If the soul (meaning Atman in this case) be infinite, there can only be ONE soul, and all ideas of various souls—you having one soul and I having another and so forth—are not real. The Real Man, therefore, is one and infinite, the omnipresent spirit. And the apparent man is only a limitation of that Real Man.[5]*

This may be approached in what could be a more accessible manner. Thus:

- The Self, atman, has no form and shape.
- It therefore *must* be present everywhere.
- The things that we think are essential for created life, *time*, *space*, and *causation* are not part of the make-up of the Self—they are part of the mind, and the Self is beyond mind.

- So if the Self is beyond mind, it must be beyond time, space, and causation.

- The Self is, therefore, infinite. How can something that is everywhere, everywhen, and without commencement or termination be other than infinite?

- And, most importantly, how could it be other than one, or universal? How can something that is infinite *not* be universal? You just cannot have two universals—it is either *uni*versal, or it is not.

- So—there is in truth only one Self (referred to as *soul* in the quote, probably for Western ears). And you and I are one and infinite, and will never cease to be, albeit we will no doubt put on a myriad different personas and appearances, both now in this life and the many others that we have had or will have. (Following the doctrine of *karma* and rebirth that is implicit in this teaching and expounded in the Bhagavad Gita and all Eastern spiritual teaching.)

So the result of this understanding is true and complete non-duality. Humankind is at its happiest when in a state of inclusivity, when egoic concerns of "what's in it for me?" are laid to rest, when the desires and fears of the mind are dispatched, and when the threefold nature of us all, truth, consciousness, and bliss, can thus be gently allowed to surface. This is the upshot of what Vivekananda, Shantananda Saraswati, and the other

Advaitins are trying to tell us. We are the true Self, big I in our initial definition, and as such have it within our power to live in a unitive state, full of bliss and contentment. To do so, however, requires that we need to ensure that our decisions are based upon truth—eschewing the egoic concerns of the ego, known as *ahankara,* which typically is driven by the two engines of desire and fear, these being the province not of universality, but of "me and mine". It is only when we re-enter this little shallow world of me and mine, when we forget the bigger picture, and when we forget who and what we really are that the trouble starts.

Advaita and Creation

"In the beginning was Brahman, with whom was the Word; and the Word was truly the supreme Brahman." These words are from the ancient Rig Veda, one of four Vedas, or spiritual teachings, in the Hindu tradition from which the mystical side of that tradition, Advaita Vedanta, evolved. The same ethos is to be found in the opening verses, probably composed 5,000 years later, of St John's Gospel in the New Testament: "in the beginning was the Word, and the Word was with God, and the Word was God. And without it was not anything made that was made." One wonders whether the writer of St John's gospel was versed in the Vedas of India. There are implications from this in terms of modernist teaching which we will look at in chapter 8, but for now we can note that this reference to a single Word, or impetus, which instigated creation is commonplace in many traditions, including the Logos to be found in the Greek, Gnostic and Hermetic output, as well as the Christian (Jesus as the "Word made flesh"). Heraclitus in the sixth century BCE advised that "having hearkened not unto me, but unto the LOGOS, it is wise to confess that all things are one". So the essence of Advaita Vedanta, that all things are "not two", is infused down the ages through the Greek tradition and what is today called Paganism, and can be discerned permeating the ancient Egyptian tradition, too, where the notion of the creative impetus being "the Word" of the Divine supreme being was established according to the pyramid texts going back to the era 1500-2000 BCE or before.

So—what is this "Word" which has such omnipotent qualities and which seems to have been so universally accepted across the great spiritual traditions of the world? Well, according to Advaita Vedanta, it is the syllable *om*. This is more of a sacred vibration than a word as such. It comprises an amalgam of three sounds, *ah*, *oo*, and *m*. This is sometimes written as *aum*, the *ah* and the *oo* merging to create *o* as in "Rome". This word has been diffused via the Egyptian tradition where the creator God is given the name "Amun", a corruption of which is now used to terminate prayer in the Christian tradition—"Amen".

There are three sounds, or energies, under the Advaita teaching, which are the means whereby creation is literally manifested, sustained, and ultimately dissolved. This may resonate with modern science, in which one of the present theories about the origin of creation is by way of a Big Bang (see chapter 9). These sounds or qualities have discrete functions in this process, so are sometimes referred to as "qualities". The Sanskrit word for them is *gunas*, so due to the difficulty of precise translation, this is the term I will use henceforth. *Rajas* is the guna of creation. It is the motive force for construction, for energy, for motivation. *Tamas* is the opposite, the guna of dissolution, darkness, of sleep or lack of energy, of holding in place. The third guna, *sattva*, is the ray of peace, rest (in a spiritual way), of serenity, well-being, and light. All three are present all the time, but normally one is pre-eminent.

One can fairly readily see when there is an oversupply of the manifestation of rajas and tamas. For example, when rajas is heavily ascendant there is an excess of energy which can manifest in anger, a worried concern for "getting a result", for lack of perception, stress, and confusion. When there is too much tamas there is inertia, obduracy, negativity, and a lack of spontaneity. But when sattva predominates, all seems peaceful and full of contentedness. One can feel these in buildings—compare the beautiful peace to be found in a "sattvic" place like a church, where people for hundreds of years have brought forth their spiritual concerns, or the "rajasic" feel of, say, a very busy open plan office, or the "tamasic" feel of a home where there is much grief, sadness, or uncontrolled despondence. The gunas are in everything and are everywhere. The weather, the seasons of the year, the ages of human beings and animals, the times of day, the mood swings of us all, the type of food we eat, and how we choose to arrange our day are all good examples of seeing the gunas in action. For example, sattva is in the ascendance about half an hour either side of sunrise and sunset, so these are propitious times in which to meditate.

Under the Advaita teaching there is one important point about this. The Self or atman remains unaffected no matter what might be the prevailing balance of these gunas. So no matter how much there is of, say, anger or the pent up energies of rajas (from which we derive the English word *rage*) or the delusions of tamas, we have it within us to transcend the guna balance prevailing at the time, and so maximise the bliss and peace of sattva. In the case of the latter, there is not an issue, but all too often it seems that an excess of either rajas or tamas causes problems. So it's a question of how we perceive things. Are we going to identify with little "me", buffeted about by life's traumas, or with big I, who basically continues unaffected by the traumas, all of which are simply witnessed without commentary? In this way one retains a blissful and steady state and a peaceful countenance.

For more on this option, listen to Shankara, in his description of the pure Self, or atman, as outlined in his *Crest Jewel of Discrimination*: "There is a self-existent Reality, which is the basis of our consciousness of ego. That Reality is the witness of the three states of our consciousness (i.e. the three gunas), and is distinct from the five bodily coverings. That Reality is the knower in all states of consciousness—waking, dreaming and dreamless sleep. It is aware of the presence of mind, and its functions. It is the ATMAN."[6] It is noteworthy that the atman is the witness of the body, mind, and so on. As witness it cannot be equated with any of this assemblage of creativity.

Shankara continues: "That reality sees everything by its own light. Noone sees it ... It pervades the universe, but no one penetrates it. It alone shines. The universe shines with its reflected light ... Its nature is eternal consciousness ... This is the atman, the Supreme Being, the ancient. It never ceases to experience infinite joy. It is always the same. It is consciousness itself."

And under the direction of Advaita Vedanta, this is a description of you and me. We are able to rise above the influences of the gunas, whether positive or negative, and so realise the fact of our ultimate oneness and, thus, encapsulate the joy of being, which is the inevitable outcome of true freedom, or detachment. How is this achieved?

- By the tool of non-attachment, or being able to rise above worldly issues.
- By working from truth.
- By meditation, thus not only gaining access to the true depth of the self, but also retaining control of the mind and its mercurial tendencies.

- By putting into practice, under direction, and with encouragement, the words of the wise. (There is a teaching known as *Dharma* in the Advaita tradition, and as *Dhamma* under Buddhism, both not dissimilar to spiritual codes of conduct issued by the Christian, Islamic, and Jewish teachings—another area of overlap of the great traditions of the world.)

- And by using the mindful techniques of attention, presence, and non-judgementalism. (These issues will be outlined further in chapter 10, entitled "Mindful Practice", at the end of this book.)

Under Advaita (as well as most other spiritual pathways), it is recommended that to embark upon such a programme, often life changing for many of us, requires help and encouragement. This will form the subject of the final phase of this book. For the moment, all we need do is rest in the knowledge that in the last resort all of us have within us the potential of true and full realisation, so that we can dwell in the land of *satchitananda*, or true peace and contentment, and not in the world of delusion. After all, if we now refer to how we described a truly wise man/woman right at the start of this book, one of the most obvious hallmarks of a wise person is that he or she is of good cheer, no matter what, and is always light and bright, seemingly able to ride the "slings and arrows of outrageous fortune" with a deft, unaffected, and detached, often humorous, take on it all.

Reality and Delusion

Much has been made above, both within this consideration of Advaita Vedanta and the other spiritual traditions, of what constitutes the ultimate reality and what, therefore, does not. The truly wise do not suffer from this problem. By deep understanding of themselves and what is real and what is merely transitory, they recognise and so are not bound by the ephemeral creation they inhabit. Under the teaching of Advaita Vedanta, this transitory manifestation is given a name—*maya*. Maya is ultimately illusion, albeit containing reality to the extent that it of necessity must contain the immanent Self. But if we proceed on the basis that *maya*, or creation as manifested, is all there is, then we deny the true self and solely inhabit the limited world of little I, or ego. This is the world of never being but always becoming. Or the world of not what I am, but what I think I am.

To move from the limited to the limitless is the stated aim and object of all the great traditions of self-awareness. In this tradition of Advaita Vedanta, the teachings of the ancient Upanishads are of the greatest importance, as is the Bhagavad Gita, in which we note that Lord Krishna is advising his devotee Arjuna that "truly this Divine Illusion of Phenomenon manifesting itself in the gunas is difficult to surmount". Well, that, I suppose, is reassuring! But the great thing about these esoteric pathways to realisation is their down-to-earth practicality and simplicity.

That does not make them easy. But Krishna continues this passage in the following terms: "Only they who devote themselves to Me, and Me alone, can accomplish it." Now it needs to be clarified that, by the term *me*, Krishna is not referring to a single ego entity called "Krishna" any more than Jesus does when describing himself in St John's gospel in the following terms: "I am the way, the truth and the life; no one comes to the Father except through me." When a realised man or an avatar of the status of a Jesus, Krishna, Buddha, or Muhammad uses the terms *I* or *me*, they are referring to the true Self, big I, which is universal.

This has been one of the most oft-encountered areas of confusion when the great religious teachings are interpreted in a narrow, literalist manner, and so it's responsible for dogmatism, misunderstanding, and religious warfare on global proportions. It is the aim of mindful philosophy to transcend such limitations and to revert to what the masters of old actually said and taught—not someone's later and almost inevitably more limited and partisan approach. That way, the essence of the teachings of any particular religion or spiritual tradition can be fully appreciated from an undiluted and transparent, uncontaminated perspective. The process is a little like a thorough cleansing of an ancient and darkly faded old master in dire need of being wiped clean and pure by those with the right understanding to do so.

So, armed with Krishna's advice to devote oneself to the true Self alone, then we have every reason to proceed along the path to full unity. That is what is referred to in the third of our four precepts we looked at to start with—the true aim of human existence. As noted above, this may necessitate some rearrangement of priorities, but those who have followed this book thus far will be familiar with that. There will need to be surrender of "worldly" values—not to negate them, but simply to let go of the attachment to them. The idea is to use the advice contained in the Isa Upanishad—"Enjoy, do not covet his property." The idea is to enjoy whatever is put our way to the full, but not to get attached to it.

So the wise fully partake of all that constitutes this magnificent and fulsome creation, but they are not bound by it. They fully enjoy and, because they've mastered the art of how to make the best and fullest use of attention and mindful living, probably enjoy to a far greater extent than is normal. But they do so in knowledge that this *maya*, this manifest creation, is ultimately nothing but a play. They have an almost childlike delight in the wondrous world we inhabit, but not as a possession or as something owned. That way lies freedom. A story is told to illustrate this, as an illustration of how, in India, one might trap a monkey. A glass jar with nuts in it is placed in the ground. This, in due course, is spied by the monkey. He thrusts his hand into the jar. He grabs a handful of nuts. His fist is now clenched, which means he cannot remove it. So he screams loudly, attracting the attentions of the monkey catcher. And all he had to do to be free was to let go. So it's a choice—either let go, or let ego.

The Context

We have explored the background to Advaita Vedanta in some depth. We have not, thus far, placed this enquiry into its context. The discussion about what constitutes reality and what is just a play assumes critical importance when we come to the realisation that the effects of this are manifested in a most direct and immediate manner in the lives of you and me. And it does so *now*. Most of the great wisdom traditions are quite unambiguous about that.

Under the principles of Advaita Vedanta, there is a carefully laid-out design which, like the Gnostic myth, is usually referred to in mythological or allegorical terms. The origin is the notion that the Absolute wanted to play. He wanted to share his creation: "I would be many." So he arranged, via the Indian pantheon of gods and sundry deities, to evolve the created universe as his plaything. By way of the evolution of creation, the ultimate result is destined to be full and complete spiritualisation of everything in that creation. The Divine essence in all living things is thereby what comes to be realised, and the being then continues as a fully integrated blissful and conscious part of the ineffable and limitless *Brahman*. But how, one may ask, is this to be achieved?

Well, not (usually) in one life. As we have already understood in our considerations of the Buddhist and Gnostic offerings, the teachings advise that human beings will come and go as and when necessary in order to learn from their specific life situations, to receive that which is owed to them, and to repay what debts, whether physical, subtle, or emotional, that might have been created in the previous life. In other words, that portion which does not decay at death assumes another body. The type, gender, profile, and location of that bodily entity will be determined by the programme he or she will have created out of what has gone before. So every being comes into the world with a bag of goodies, both positive and negative, as a result of what took place previously and what is now needed to fulfil one's destiny (known in Sanskrit as *sanskara*). The pack of cards is, therefore, not random. It is self-created. Hence, the wide disparity of apparent fortune, talents, "accidents" of birth, and the like.

Naturally, we can have only very limited, if any, access to knowledge of past lives; otherwise, the whole system could dissolve. This is because there would be an unacceptable influence upon individual free will, which could in turn lead to "unfinished business" such as personal or family relationships in need of repair being unable to be properly seen without angst from the past. But if one can view this dispassionately, it can readily be appreciated that it does at least allow the possibility for a rational, humane and just resolution providing the means of finishing the unfinished business, whether personal or on a wider scale. It can also place in context the otherwise inexplicable manifestations of apparent injustices such as premature death, illness, unequal distribution of wealth and many more. This is essentially the law of cause and effect, implementing the biblical statement "As ye sow, so shall ye reap." In the Advaita tradition, this is referred to as the law of *karma*. Karma is a Sanskrit word which literally means "action". Other traditions where this doctrine is to be found include Buddhism, and Gnosticism amongst others.

The Bhagavad Gita provides much advice about the concept of action, including consideration as to the intended beneficiary of an action ("me" or the universal "self"?). Then there is the purpose of the action—is it on the small scale of just for my benefit, or is there a bigger picture? And what about the result? It is one thing to undertake an action because one has a preconceived notion of an end result and quite another to undertake the action selflessly, just for the sake of the action. As stated in the Bhagavad Gita: "Perform all your actions with your mind concentrated upon the Divine, renouncing attachment, and looking upon success and failure with an equal eye. Spirituality implies equanimity."

It might be worth clarifying at this juncture that the idea of "renouncing attachment" does not mean renouncing love or care. The opposite is the case. For example, if a brain surgeon embarking upon a critical and complex operation were to "emote" and become all dysfunctional, then what use is he as a brain surgeon? The reasons for which he spent years training have not gone away—the need to care for others and the like—but at that precise moment, what is needed is dispassionate, unattached one-pointed attention to the job at hand. So, with this in mind, and living in such a way that we retain our reason whilst allowing our innate love and care to motivate us, we can address all our issues and retain steadiness of being.

Ultimately, according to the Gita, if we continue along this path living a disciplined life and a life full of joy and peace, there will come a time when we will no longer require to incarnate, and so lengthen the cycle of birth/ death/rebirth, and so on. The choice to do so is ours. This may require much application and can appear a hard task. But "when the student is ready, the master appears", and we need a certain amount of faith to embark upon this task. When all is considered, all we are doing with this is to renounce anything that is not wholly related to our essential threefold nature of truth/being, consciousness, and true happiness or bliss.

CHAPTER 7

NON-DUALITY ALL OVER THE WORLD

We say that a person is a person through other persons. We don't come fully formed into the world. We learn how to think, how to walk, how to speak, how to behave, indeed how to be human, from other human beings. We need other human beings to be human. We are made for togetherness, we are made for family, for fellowship, to exist in a tender network of interdependence.[1]

Desmond Tutu

Thus far we have followed the golden thread of mindful philosophy through some of the great global traditions of the world—Christianity and its derivatives, mystical Islam by way of the Sufis, the Greek and Egyptian traditions, Buddhism, Taoism, and Advaita Vedanta. Before moving on to some of the more recent advocates of non-duality, I want to consider the extent to which this teaching can be discerned in Africa and in other areas not necessarily or often associated with a history of spiritual teaching in the Western world. To be an effective and credible force for the common good, mindful philosophy has to be seen to be accessible to all human beings in all circumstances, and for all time. Humankind places itself under needless suffering and angst if it departs from the unitive and wholesome approach which constitutes non-duality and substitutes instead a mean-spirited, fear-driven, and ego-imbued roadway by adherence to the limited, the selfish, and the possessive.

One can see this by reference to one's circle of influence, or family. Indeed, one may truthfully enquire, Who is my family? Am I on my own? Or do I admit others to my area of care and concern, like my parents, partner, or siblings? Does or should it end there? Or should I include my mother-in-law? Or maybe those cousins I really don't see a great deal of? They are in my family after all, aren't they? And what about all those folk at the wedding last year? Never seen any of them before. But they're all now in my family, aren't they? Well, if they are all in my family and I hardly know them, what about my friends who I know well, some for many years? Surely, they deserve to be included in my family? And what about my colleagues at work with whom I probably spend more time than anyone else? And if they are all *in*, it's getting hard to see who is *out*.

It's been said that the wise person considers the whole world to be her or his family. And that is indeed the essence of non-duality. It's how one perceives one's fellow being. The wise do not see other because all they see is one. They can but perceive unity, and if we are to believe the mystics, that unitive state is utterly and comprehensively blissful. One can take this line of reasoning a stage further by considering the world beyond "family". What is the appropriate unit of care? Should it stay at the immediate family level, or should it include my city or neighbourhood? Or should it go out further to include my country? What about race—should I have care just for my race, or can I not acknowledge the humanity in all races? Does it stop there? Why can't it include all peoples throughout the universe? And if the answer to that is yes, what are the implications for "little I", the ego, now that it is a lone voice striving for its very survival in a world where love and care are acknowledged as universal human characteristics, unbowed by time, place, nation, or caste?

Well, in the twenty-first century these are huge and ever-pressing issues. The mindful philosopher, coming from a background of spirituality, has to engage with them. The engagement, however, is created out of love, which by its very nature is inclusive, all-embracing, and compassionate, provided its natural purity is not contaminated by ego concerns and possessiveness. In other words, to use the words of Advaita, love under *sattva* will provide and sustain a world of purity and lucidity, of well-being, truth, and contentedness. Love distorted under excess *rajas* can easily become jealous, worried about possessions, and so become scheming and devious. Love under *tamas,* if in excess, will become delusional and can then manifest in a dour obduracy, and misapprehension, thinking wrong to be right and vice versa.

Ubuntu

The quotation from Desmond Tutu above is taken from the African tradition of *Ubuntu*. This is a Bantu word which can be loosely translated as "humanity", or humanity towards others. So it implies the notion of what it means to be human. And it requires appraisal of just what is needed to create the appropriate environment for human beings to grow and flourish in a contented and inclusive manner—"the belief in a universal bond of sharing that connects all humanity". To that extent it espouses a code of conduct, or ethical stance—"I am well, happy, and content if you are well, happy, and content." We can only grow and evolve as humans to the extent that we acknowledge and respect the humanity in so-called others. In fact, we do not, under Ubuntu, really accept the notion of "other" at all. The idea of community is fundamental in African philosophy, and that needs to be recognised in how individual human relationships are conducted. If, for example, an individual has no hesitation in looking after someone in great need, whether known to him or her or not, then one could describe that individual as having Ubuntu. It's a state of being. And in that manner, if one "has" Ubuntu, one would be described as a full or developed person, endowed with a spirituality or energy conducive to care for the common good and the well-being of all. Desmond Tutu said, "My humanity is caught up, is inextricably bound up, in what is yours."[2] So Tutu saw no conflict or tension between the indigenous African teaching coming from

Ubuntu, and the teaching of Jesus Christ, in his capacity as archbishop of Cape Town.

Ubuntu is the driver of unity and reconciliation and as such was espoused by Nelson Mandela. The Truth and Reconciliation Commission was established upon such principles, and has been referred to by many contemporary African and non-African luminaries since the passing of Mandela in the hope that such teachings could enlighten and sustain the post-apartheid era in South Africa.

The idea is that the universe basically comprises a set of interrelating forces—forces interacting with other forces in a universal force field, as opposed to things reacting with other things. This force field runs through and permeates the whole of the created universe. Rather like the teachings of Steiner, and to be found in many of the great teachings from Advaita Vedanta and Buddhism to the Quakers/Shakers, which form part of the Christian offering today, this life force is held to exist in all parts of creation from the mineral kingdom of rocks, through the vegetable kingdom, and through the animal kingdom to humankind. This life force is, therefore, the fundamental substratum of the whole of creation. And it unites everyone and everything of which it is composed. This includes us all, and indeed it is held that we as "individuals" only exist at all insofar as we are part of the created interrelationships between us all and creation. In this manner, there is no such thing as a separate self. There is no separation between the individual and the greater community. The notion of community is fundamental, and the basic building block of which Ubuntu society is established. One identifies not as oneself as an individual, nor others as individuals, but as members of the community, first and foremost.

This outlook creates a need for cooperation and discussion, rather than resorting to power politics. Consensus is the order of the day, requiring patient discussion designed to lead to unanimity as the goal in the dealings of everyday life.

The Ubuntu tradition holds that one joins the human family at birth but does not leave it at death. In this way, ancestors are considered as part of the greater community, by virtue of the unextinguished life force of which everything is composed. Taken right through to its logical conclusion, it is clear from this that ultimately the whole of humanity is interrelated and is one entity—an exemplary manifestation of non-duality. This is continued into the ethical system which accompanies Ubuntu thought, in that human development and evolution is not by way of the individual as an egoic self-centred entity, but is determined by the extent to which the community has become enhanced by one's life. In other words, it is a question of becoming more human. And one becomes more and more human as time goes by, and as experience of life so ordains. Thus, there is great reverence in the Ubuntu world for age. The life force can never be extinguished, which is why there is so much reverence both for the elders of society, and those who have passed on.

The Indigenous Traditions

There is a homely wisdom to be found amongst the many folk traditions which have always inhabited the earth. Sometimes this can be found in myth and legend, in so-called fairy tales, which tend to harbour much of great spiritual worth, hidden within the recesses of their imagery. And sometimes it can be manifested in reverence for the earth, for Gaia, and implied by such notions as Shangri-La, the Celtic destination of the eternally youthful known as Tir nan Og, and many other similar traditions, including those of Native America and the Australian Aborigines. Whilst many of these may not, at least overtly, exhibit an obvious trend of non-duality, there does seem to be a link between them all based upon the acknowledgement of the existence of a supreme being or substratum with whom and in whom the "soul" (or "Self") of the individual is destined to unite. I believe that in this way, the golden thread of mindful philosophy makes its presence felt, and all that the mindful philosopher needs is to keep mind and heart open and receptive, laying on one side whatever formulation of spiritual teaching he or she may be familiar with, or will have been educated by, so as to appreciate the depth and profundity of these "folk" traditions. Such traditions have also enriched humanity by their art, poetry, dance, stories, and culture, but for these to be appreciated, the recipient must first lay down his or her preconceptions as to what they *ought* to be like, and so enter the present moment and in a mindful non-judgemental manner, and so just listen/watch, or partake as appropriate.

The Native American Tradition

This is a difficult area to appraise, but it does seem that underlying the practices of the many and varied tribes, at least those who have aspirations to evolve, is a fundamental reverence for spirituality and the need to walk with the Great Spirit. As has been already mentioned, it is the victors who get to write the history lessons, not the vanquished. One wonders what might have gone astray since the Americas were occupied by the white man. Consider this well-known quotation from Chief Seattle:

> *The President in Washington sends word that he wishes to buy our land. But how can you buy and sell the sky, the land? The idea is strange to us. Every part of this Earth is sacred to my people, every shining pine needle, every sandy shore, every mist in the dark woods, every meadow is holy in the memory and experience of my people. We are all part of the Earth, and it is part of us. The perfumed flowers are our sisters. The bear, the deer, the great eagle, these are our brothers. Each ghostly reflection in the clear lakes tells of memories and events in the life of my people. The water's murmur is the voice of my father's father If we sell our land, remember the air is precious to us, that the air shares its spirit*

with all the life it supports. The wind that gave our grandfather his first breath receives his last sigh. This we know. The earth does not belong to man: man belongs to the Earth. All things are connected like the blood that connects us all. Man did not weave the web of life, he is merely a strand in it. Whatever he does to the web he does to himself. Your destiny is a mystery to us. What will happen when the buffalo are all slaughtered? What will happen when the secret corners of the forest are heavy with the scent of many men, and the view of the ripe hills is blotted with talking wires? The end of living and the beginning of survival. When the last red man vanishes with his wildness, and his memory is only a shadow of a cloud moving across the prairie, will these shores still be here? Will there be any spirit of my people left? We love the Earth as the new—born loves its mother's heart beat. So if we sell our land, love it as we have loved it; care for it as we have cared for it. Hold in mind the memory of the land as it is when you receive it. Hold in your mind the memory of the land as it is when you receive it. Preserve the land for all children, and love it as God loves us all. One thing we know. There is only one God. No man, be he red man or white man, can be apart. We are brothers after all.[3]

Now what type of individual, and what type of culture which produced him, does this illustrate? How can that clearly expressed notion of interconnectedness exist without a fundamental knowledge of the essence, or unity that unites all humanity? And is there not a fundamental non-duality exemplified by the reverence for all creation and all humans, red or white, by this beautiful excerpt?

The Native American belief system appears to depend upon a spirituality, which under some traditions involves walking along a "Red Road" of spirituality, or life development. There is a well-defined philosophical background outlined in the "seven philosophies", as outlined by Native American elders as to how the subjects of women, children, family, community, mother earth, spiritual growth and himself should be perceived by Native American men. There are seven similar philosophies for Native American women. Their teaching was basically experiential, or embraced "phenomenology". The seven philosophies can briefly be summarised as follows:

1) To the women. Given the ultimate sacredness of life, the capacity of the woman to reproduce life means that all men need to treat women with dignity and respect, and to not abuse them. Women are the foundation of the family and so must be treated in a sacred manner.

2) To the children. Children must be given time, prayers, and proper education, because adults are the caretakers of children for the creator. Adults need to behave as role models.

3) To the family. The family is the home for right teachings to be availed, from grandparents and parents. In this way, the child

will reflect the behaviour of the parents, ensuring that the family becomes a crucible for strength, mental health, and well-being.

4) To the community. A sense of belonging is essential for health and well-being, so the individual is required to give time to develop friendships and to share talents, for the benefit of successive generations.

5) To the earth. Mother Earth is the highest teacher, so must be treated with honour and respect. Land, water, and air must be passed on in an uncontaminated state for the benefit of successive generations. The unity and interconnectedness of all beings, all things, all forms of life is a paramount philosophy, and this depends upon implementing the natural law.

6) To the Creator. Spiritual values must be implemented in the life; nothing can be gained without the inert participation of the Great Spirit. This means walking the "Red Road" of life; of spiritual growth, whether one is Christian or not. Time and commitment are required daily for spiritual development.

7) To myself. I need to consider what my values must be if I am to evolve. This means walking with the Great Spirit. Mental discipline and a positive attitude are what I need to bring to bear. I need to examine my strengths and weaknesses, my attributes, and where improvements are needed, on a daily basis. My life must be principled.

These principles could equally well be articulated in any or all of the great world traditions we have already examined. They illustrate how the mindful philosophy practitioner needs to keep focussed and adopt a practical attitude to the day-to-day stuff of life. The need to appraise one's own life could have come from a Platonic instruction, and the significance of the world of nature is akin to the Ubuntu practices we have been looking at.

The Native American tradition was, therefore, able to demonstrate a considerable degree of sophistication, and whilst caution is needed because of the many varying belief systems of the various tribes, the inclusiveness both of the philosophical stance and of the dignified reaction to a most pressing situation shown by Chief Seattle indicates a culture certainly embracing of unitive principles.

Shamanism and Other Indigenous Traditions

It is tempting to draw conclusions about many other indigenous peoples in the same way, but this must be treated warily. Many of these are similar to shamanism, which evolved initially from Siberia, and about which there is currently considerable discussion and disagreement within that community. Shamanism is often associated with healing properties, many times involving the healer going into trance by means of drumming or other inducements, and able thereby to heal whatever problem exists in the soul or subconscious of the sufferer. It has similarities with the Native American tradition insofar as there is great reverence for the natural world. Shamanism is one of the earliest spiritual traditions of the planet, and was associated with hunter/gatherer communities, but is presently undergoing something of a revival via the New Age and other schools of thought, including neo-shamanism. Whilst this is somewhat contentious, what is interesting from the perspective of mindful philosophy is the fact that deeply embedded in many thinking people today is a desire to accommodate nature, to respect and nurture her, and to, as it were, "be at one" with the natural world. There are many pathways to the top of the philosophical mountain, and shamanism and allied traditions can be of great assistance in turning the materialist and pedestrian acquisitive values of the twenty-first century towards something far more wholesome and inclusive. The teaching of Mindful Philosophy is rooted in unity, and the direction of travel of shamanism in its many and various manifestations does seem basically to be inclusive and fully embracing of diversity.

One of the most significant areas of communality which to my mind show light on a non-dual and inclusive approach is through sound, singing, rhythm, and dance. These are strong features in the indigenous folk history of many cultures, including the Native American. Folk music has a plaintive, almost other-worldly quality about it at times. And who could fail to be moved by the Abbots Bromley Horn Dance, an English Morris dance, with its hauntingly beautiful tune and dignified almost stately dance movements? The native traditions all across the world have much to teach the sophisticated and intellectually driven Western world.

The Songlines of the Aborigines

One of the most well-known examples of this is the Australian aboriginal tradition, which tells of the idea of songlines. Songlines are routes across the landscape, sky, or wherever demarcating the pathways taken by creator entities, which they undertake as they enter their "dreaming" mode. These pathways may be recognised physically on the ground and can be accessed by chanting the songs in the appropriate rhythmic manner. This was how the native Aborigine would navigate his way across the arid Australian wastelands. To ensure that the system works required commitment to the relevant spirit being, or totem—another overlap with the native Americans. So the songline forms a concept of the direction of travel of these beings and so can be communicated directly to their adherents. Indeed, this was how everything became made manifest—by singing out whatever came their way, be it mountains and rocks, water sources, vegetation and plants, animals and birds.

And this creation by singing out strikes a chord with much of modern science, which I will consider in due course, but for the moment it is worth noting that the New Zealand biologist and philosopher Darryl Reanney in his book *Music of the Mind* reveals an insight in which songlines can be seen not simply as a piece of somewhat remote indigenous culture but as something embedded and hardwired into the make-up of us all. This is why they are of interest in a study of non-duality. The idea is, according to Reanney, that because we might find a piece of music to be "moving", we might almost automatically wish to move to it—to dance. It is well known that certain drumbeat rhythms can lead to trance, as exemplified by the Sufis and many cultures. Reanney says, "Thus was dancing born in olden times, as a sacred ritual to make manifest in movement the mystery of the world's unfolding."

Reanney's thesis is based upon the notion of "knowing" being explicable as a concept in a scientific manner using quantum physics. Knowing is a function of recognition (recognition, to know again). Knowing is, as it were, held in a reservoir of "collective knowing" which may be likened to the collective unconscious of Jung. We all have access to this reservoir, but only to the extent that we are aware or have evolved along a particular route. Reanney believes that the knowing is actually definable as a series of quantum waves, which "resonate" only when the subject (for example, the mind of the pupil) and the object (for example, the mind of the teacher) are in synchronicity, or as he puts it, in "wave form". Knowing in this manner can be availed simply by waves—not necessarily by use of words at all.

Resonance is something with which most of us will be familiar with, and this is something that is much referred to by the mystics, in that they advise that in this mode the seer *becomes* the sight, the thinker *becomes* the thought, and the knower *becomes* the known. We will be considering the important contribution of modern science including the data from quantum waves later, but for the moment the point is simply this. "Knowing" is recognition. Recognition is wave resonance, which are functions of waves in the subtle world. This is why certain reiterative music can induce altered states of consciousness. And following the evidence from quantum theory, which is that waves will become particles of matter once consciousness is applied to them, one can understand that, to quote Reanney, in relation to the Aborigines: "an imaginal song may become a physical structure, the "LOWER—ENERGY" (i.e. the physical world) knowing may remake the higher in its own image. Almost literally. So, at its limit and under the right conditions, KNOWING MAY CREATE A WORLD, just as the Aborigines have said." So, "knowing is the original software of consciousness itself." And this process is what he believes can be described as *songlines*. Indeed, his theory is that our "souls" can be described as the "songlines of our lives".

Myth and Legend

One of the lessons we can learn from the indigenous traditions is the value of what is contained in myth and legend, which is something we touched upon earlier. Fairy tales tend to exhibit a common background in that they can be taken on at least two levels. In fact, this applies not just to fairy tales but to virtually all spiritually inclined literature. This is something which Dante referred to in his *Divine Comedy* in which four levels of meaning are outlined.

There is the *literal* level, so that one places simply a literal interpretation upon what is read—the creation was literally created in seven days, or the battle outlined in the Bhagavad Gita literally took place as described therein.

Then there is the *moral* level—the story is interpreted to reveal a truth about right and wrong, good and bad, and whatever of the manifold human behavioural options the story is describing. The idea of moral law can be introduced at this stage.

Thirdly is the *allegorical* level—the tale is describing by way of symbol and signs the existence of something of far greater depth than just a pretty story. The "road to Jerusalem" is not just a highway from one place to another, but a route to self-realisation—it actually represents one's life journey with all its ups and downs, rather as illustrated in the tale we had earlier about the man who went from Baghdad to Cairo in search of the missing treasure.

And finally is the *"anagogical"* level, in which something of the world of the spiritual—the means whereby the individual may move from individuality and separation towards unity and integration with his or her true essence and so realise who and what he or she really is. In this way, we can fully appraise not only fairy tales and traditional legends but also parables from teachers such as Jesus (may those who have ears to hear, hear, and those whom have eyes, see).

Where does this take us so far as the traditional myths and legends of folk and indigenous cultures are concerned? Well, modern research reveals a common direction of travel discernible in most fairy tales to greater or lesser extent. The author and teacher Ann Gadd has written an ingenious and fascinating book entitled *Climbing the Beanstalk* in which she outlines the existence of a sevenfold evolution of the hero/heroine, each phase exemplifying particular character types or *archetypes,* and in the process of which he or she undergoes life experiences which can be related to the *chakras.*[4]

Archetypes are a Jungian feature and easily recognisable in daily life—for example, the "dodgy geezer", the "computer nerd", "mother earth", the "smooth operator", the "lady of easy virtue", the "slick businessman", the "financial wizard", the "scientific boffin", and so on. They are a means of conveying an idea to illustrate patterns of behaviour within various types of people. In fairy tales, these include the wicked stepmother, the noble prince, the beautiful daughter, and so on. By engaging with them we can become a whole person, see the bigger picture, recognise the archetype for what it is, and so progress along our spiritual path. The chakras are subtle energy centres in the body—seven of them ranging from the base one, the root chakra at the tailbone of the spine,to the highest one at the crown of the head.

For Ann Gadd, the typical fairy tale is an illustration of how the human being, whether he or she realises it or not, is involved upon a journey from gross to fine—from incomprehension to realisation. This comprises the innate desire sustained within us all to reunite with the Divine, to climb the ladder of Jacob. No one knows who first penned the traditional fairy tales or quite how old they are. Like folk music, they are a continuing seam of ancient culture. Ann Gadd has a marvellous way of perceiving how various seemingly quite disparate world cultures can shed light together if their data can be accepted allegorically and "anagogically." The tales are the means whereby deep seated spiritual wisdom can be availed by the common man/woman who may otherwise not have any particular reason or aptitude to study such matters. This is very helpful as a tool for the mindful philosopher.

Not all traditional fairy tales include all seven layers, but some, such as Jack and the Beanstalk and Cinderella, do. Briefly, at stage one there will be some form of betrayal, tragedy, or loss to spoil the hero's life – "once upon a time…..". The archetype here is that of victim. This can be seen as the catalyst to send us out upon a quest or journey towards spiritual fulfilment. So off we go, and indeed we can now enter stage two, Divine help, in which help is availed from a Divine source, such as a fairy godmother, or in real life, maybe a meeting with a teacher, a book, some chance occurrence, and so on. This could involve personal tragedy or loss—it can sometimes take appalling experiences if all else fails, and we persist in refusing to engage with truth and, as it were, insisting upon keeping our "head down". The sacral chakra is operating, the archetype being the martyr or servant, and so the journey is commenced. The servant can be seen as self-serving,or as serving others, such as some powerful figure (archetype empress). In this way, we are now on a journey or quest to which there is no return and from which there is no escape (e.g., dark forest).

We now enter stage three, the quest, where the real work starts, in which the hero/heroine requires all available courage, personal integrity, and fortitude, sometimes having to undertake being thrown out of the kingdom or another similarly dire situation. The situation is symbolised by the warrior archetype, and operates from the third chakra, the solar plexus. In real life, this may be seen as needing to confront our own demons, to operate away from our comfort zone and confronting areas of our make-up that perhaps we would rather leave hidden. In this way, we grow and become strong and ultimately happy in our own skins. This leads to the fourth stage, integration, governed by the heart chakra and the lover or actor archetype. The tale might feature a love interest and marriage. But there are important lessons to be learnt—like self-acceptance and integration of our male aspects with our female.

Typically, the tale now moves on, and in stage five, the beast is slain, the wicked witch is boiled in oil, or the evil queen ends up in a barrel of snakes! The symbolism of this is the slaying of the ego, the small self. Little I is no longer going to trouble us. Unless this takes place, we can make no further spiritual progress. Truth is what we need. The chakra operating is that of the throat, and the archetype that of the magician or alchemist. The alchemist knows how to purify, to change from base metal to gold—in this case to relinquish our attachments and ego-based desires and aversions so that they can be replaced with pure consciousness, love, and contentment.

There are two stages left—the sixth is "crossing the abyss", in which we are put to the final test in which some kind of "dark night of the soul" is needed to be experienced. The process of entering the Divine realm has of necessity to be preceded by relinquishing the gross, mental, and subtle realms, and this has to be undertaken alone. The chakra is that of the brow, symbolised by the intellectual/intuitive archetype. We must summon up all our strength if we are not to relapse back to our former existence. This is accomplished by the surrender of our individual will to that of the Divine.

And then? Well, we will have become united with the Divine, from which in truth we were never really severed in the first place. Enlightenment or spiritual union will have been obtained. The seventh chakra is the crown, and the archetype, the Master. And so truly we will live "happily ever after". Ann Gadd's book contains a far more detailed exposure of these ideas and includes a number of appraisals of various tales from the perspective of what is referred to as mindful philosophy in this book. The book is thoroughly recommended.

CHAPTER 8

MINDFUL PHILOSOPHY—THE TWENTIETH AND TWENTY-FIRST CENTURIES

The realisation of the Non-dual traditions is uncompromising: there is only Spirit, there is only God, there is only Emptiness in all its wonder. All the good and all the evil, the very best and the very worst, the upright and the degenerate—each and all are radically perfect manifestations of spirit precisely as they are. There is nothing but God, nothing but the Goddess, nothing but spirit in all directions, and not a grain of sand, nor a speck of dust, is more or less spirit than any other.

Ken Wilber, The Eye of the Spirit[1]

There is no reaching the Self. If Self were to be reached, it would mean that the Self is not here and now and that it is yet to be obtained. What is got afresh will also be lost. So it will be impermanent. What is not permanent is not worth striving for. So I say the Self is not reached. You are the Self, you are already that.

Ramana Maharshi, Collected Works[2]

The two quotations above are pointing to the same truth—that you *are* that which you seek once you have embarked upon the quest for realisation. The quotations exemplify the fusion of Eastern and Western cultures in this way. In fact, the duality of East and West is demonstrably non-existent when perceived through the lens of mindful philosophy or non-duality. Indeed, the more one looks for evidence of the golden thread of non-duality, the more one finds it. This is despite what has tended to be a hostile environment in which religions and philosophies of a literalist or fundamentalist perspective have tended to gain favour in both the political and "spiritual" establishment in much of the nineteenth and twentieth centuries.

This, however, is not something that is going to continue, at least not in quite such a dogmatic and unresponsive manner. We are going through a fundamental reappraisal, and it's happening right now. We are emerging from the zodiacal or astrological period of Pisces in which the norm, at least in the West, has been directed by the Christian perspective, albeit manifesting in a myriad differing forms and structures. We are entering a brave new world—that of the age of Aquarius, in which it seems that there has to be much destruction and sweeping away of the former order so that the new regime can bed down. As Tennyson so succinctly put it, "The old order changeth yielding place to new." What this means is that as this book is being composed in the second decade of the twenty-first century, the world seems to be being shaken at the roots as formerly established principles, customs, and lifestyles are being mercilessly questioned and investigated, not least by an uncomprehending younger generation, appalled by what is condoned by the powerful elite of various political hues in the name of religion.

All, however, is not lost. There will, I believe, come a time when this destruction will be seen to have been not only inevitable but also desirable. There is a great deal to be optimistic about. All over the Western world (and quite possibly the Eastern as well), there are "green shoots" of new spiritual teaching. Most of these have no particular genre to inhabit—no axe to grind, as it were. Authors and philosophers abound—those that have provided inspiration for this book include Eckhart Tolle, Deepak Chopra, Ken Wilber, Darryl Reanney, Malcolm Hollick, Timothy Freke, Robert Holden, Aldous Huxley, Paul Brunton, Rupert Spira, and Ann Gadd to name just a few, and whose contributions, so far as this book is concerned, are outlined below. All offer an inclusive, undogmatic, and experiential approach and all, to greater or lesser extent, espouse what I have described as mindful philosophy in these pages. Truly, they are products of our age, and the study of what they are offering provides the mindful philosophy student with a veritable library of philosophical works of the highest order. The common ground across them all is an acknowledgement of the simple non-dual truth that there is no separation between all of us, and that the goal is realisation of the single non-dual substratum which comprises the Self—big I. It is, of course, not the aim of this book to provide a treatise on each of these and the many others which I have not mentioned. The reader may well wish to investigate specific areas of mindful philosophy according to taste and proclivity. But looked at as a composite whole, we do need to acknowledge the importance and extent of what has come about to broaden the spiritual horizons of us all in such a short time.

How has this come about? Well, I want now to regress a little and look at some of the teachers from the nineteenth century by way of the Transcendentalists in the United States, certain English teachers such as James Allen and Richard Jefferies, theosophy, and culminating in what is described by Aldous Huxley as the perennial philosophy. We can then consider some specifics, such as the influence on a global basis of teachers such as Nisargadatta Maharaj, Ramana Maharshi and his followers, and the notion of what is sometimes referred to as *Neo-Advaita*. There is not least the enormous influence across the globe of the introduction of mantra-based meditation which emanates from the "holy tradition" under guidance of Shankara outlined in chapter 6, by way of teachings and instruction as well as meditation techniques from the "Shankaracharyas"— teachers of the way of Shankara, now easily availed on a world wide basis, courtesy of various "practical philosophy" schools. But, first, let us take a look at what was taking place in the English-speaking world during the nineteenth century, because this was the preparation for worldwide philosophical developments later.

Transcendentalists and English Mysticism in the Nineteenth Century

The philosophical garden which is manifesting the green shoots now was planted during the latter years of the nineteenth century. There were a number of channels of enquiry, partially based upon data coming out of the British Raj in India, partially from researches of an esoteric nature driven by a refusal not to be constricted by the straitjackets of formalised religion, and partially by scientific and technological research including the researches of Charles Darwin, which was channelling the thinking of the spiritual and religious establishment of the time. Add to this the ever-growing influences from the far flung outposts of the British Empire introducing concepts like tolerance, spiritual growth, and even ideas such as reincarnation, then it was quite clear that the time was right for investigation. There were many and various endeavours, one of the principal of which was the establishment initially in the United States but ultimately on a global basis of theosophy. A few years earlier had seen the emergence of a broad based quasi-religious movement known as Transcendentalism.

Transcendentalism can be seen as a natural derivative of English romanticism, in which poets like Robert Browning and William Wordsworth had exhibited a marked spiritual tendency which, rather than following the narrow church-led belief system of the day, embraced a far more inclusive and introspective approach. Also formative in the transcendentalist offering was the German philosophical tradition, notably Immanuel Kant, and, most significantly, the Advaita teaching from India. The most well-known exponent is probably Ralph Waldo Emerson, who had a marked unitive leaning in his books and publications. He coined the word *oversoul*, and in his outline on "American Transcendentalism" is to be found the following: "There is One Man—present to all particular men only; and that you must take the whole society to find the whole man."(from the talk "The American Scholar" in 1837). The idea was to come to the understanding that although manifesting as an individual, human beings needed to realise their oneness with the Divine essence by way of their containment within of an aspect of the oversoul. This is surely another example of not either/or but both/and, the notion that we have considered earlier.

Or from one of his essays, the following is a description of what today we might call wisdom, or understanding, named "reason" in the quotation: "There is one mind common to all individual men. Every man is an inlet to the same and to all of the same. He that is once admitted to the right of reason is made a freeman of the whole estate. What Plato thought, he may think: what a saint has felt, he may feel; what at any time has befallen any man, he can understand. Who hath access to this universal mind is a party to all that is or can be done, for this is the only and sovereign agent."[3] This has a definite feeling of Indian detachment about it and offers a way of understanding free of judgement or the need for compliance—just surrendering of one's ideas is all that is needed to be "freeman of the whole estate". This Indian influence is perhaps even more marked in Henry Thoreau, who let it be known that "in the morning I bathe my intellect in the stupendous and cosmogonal philosophy of the Bhagavat Geeta".

This deep and broad outlook continued by way of the verse of Walt Whitman, and is still a force to be engaged with in certain aspects of both American and European liberalism, including the Quaker or Shaker tradition. Indeed, it is something of an irony that this broad and tolerant philosophy started to gain acceptance in the East of the United States just at the time the "white man" was busily doing his best to eradicate not dissimilar aspects of unitive teaching practiced by the "red man" in other parts of the country. But towards the end of the nineteenth century, non-dual teaching took another turn by way of the advent of theosophy.

There were a number of compatible non-dualistic thinkers on the other side of the Atlantic at the time. A mid-nineteenth-century English philosopher called James Allen wrote a beautiful little book entitled *As a Man Thinketh*. Basically, the book is an empowering statement of the fact that only by seeing the mind as an instrument which can be used for good or ill may we rise above it. "By the right choice and true application of thought, man ascends to the Divine Perfection; by the abuse and wrong application of thought, he descends below the level of the beast."[4] So there we have it. Divine perfection or utter bestiality—the choice lies before us all.

In another passage, Allen likens the mind to a garden. Humankind can tend the garden of the mind, "weeding out all the wrong, useless and impure thoughts, and cultivating towards perfection the flowers and fruits of right, useful and pure thoughts".[5] In this manner, one can become the "master gardener of the soul". This is something very akin to what is today better known as mindfulness, which is the practical application of the philosophy teaching.

Finally, to exemplify just how all-embracing is the teaching of non-duality, the English nature writer Richard Jefferies wrote a most entrancing book called *The Story of My Heart*, in which he describes his need for "soul life". He is not a philosopher as such, nor an academic. His tale of the heart is spoken from the heart, and in doing so carries a ring of certainty and authority about it. Here is a sample taken from his musings upon lying upon an ancient 2,000-year-old tumulus in the heart of the Wiltshire Downs:

> *It is eternity now. I am in the midst of it. It is about me in the sunshine; I am in it, as the butterfly floats in the light laden air. Nothing has to come; it is now. Now is eternity; now is the immortal life. Here this moment, by this tumulus, on earth, now; I exist in it. The years, the centuries, the cycles are absolutely nothing;*

it is only a moment since this tumulus was raised; in a thousand
years more it will still be only a moment. To the soul there is no
past and no future; all is and will be ever, in now.[6]

Our golden thread of mindful philosophy can be discerned in these passages. To come up with writings so lucid and transparent exemplifies a deep surrender of "mind stuff". The Jefferies quote might equally have come from a modern mindfulness practitioner, an Indian text, or a Zen Buddhist tale. To get to the place wherein we can both write and properly read with understanding such passages requires that we too need to enter some kind of equanimity of being, characterised by cleansing the mind as James Allen has recommended, and then, as Emerson has so succinctly reminded us, we can feel and empathize with exactly the same thought processes as the author. Indeed, it is my hope that you, the reader, are doing exactly that now!

We now need to broaden our horizons and take a look at the global dimension, for at the end of the nineteenth century and the start of the twentieth, there were philosophical cataclysms about to take place, the reverberations from which we have yet to fully assimilate.

Theosophy

Theosophy started as a group of seekers in 1875 investigating philosophical doctrines, including the so-called occult, and other data of a mystical genre, under the leadership initially of Helena Blavatsky. The word incorporates the Greek words *theo,* meaning the divine, and *sophia,* so literally means "divine wisdom". One can trace the word back hundreds of years—which, as its subject matter is of universal significance is perhaps unsurprising. Included in the theosophical output was not only material deriving from the Vedas of India, but also from Jewish mysticism known as the Kabballah, or tree of life. Gnostic principles of inclusivity and mysticism are to be found, and theosophy is referred to in a number of later European teachings, notably those of Jacob Boehme, to which we made reference above in chapter 4. I believe that despite some somewhat bizarre offshoots in the latter nineteenth and early twentieth centuries that the essence of theosophy, at least as I understand it, being an endeavour to make available the truth about human beings on an inclusive and universal basis, makes it essentially a non-dual system and so compliant with our four precepts with which we started this book. A motto was produced: "There is no religion higher than truth."

There were a number of derivatives, including Christian theosophy, and some authorities include the mystery teachings of ancient Egypt and the Neoplatonists that we considered in chapters 4 and 5, within the theosophy remit. Objectives included the investigation of the true potential within the human being, natural law, the study of comparative religion, and a general move towards human inclusivity without dogma. As is virtually universally the case in non-dual or esoteric teaching, meditation is fundamental. There are said to be three basic tenets or areas of investigation:

i) The trinity comprising the Divine, the human, and nature. These three unite under the higher mind via which the Divine nature of the human can be realised as integral with humanity, and because nature is also infused with life, and so the Divine likewise.

ii) The great truths of creation are accessible via myth and legend to an extent greater than by crude informative process. All emanates ultimately from a mythic or imaginary starting point.

iii) The human being has the capacity to access any and all levels of experience, and so realise "full awakening".

These will by now resonate with a degree of familiarity, as they are repeated and assimilated to greater or lesser extent in all of our areas of research thus far. The theosophists encoded their teachings in seven emblems or symbols, including from Vedic India the true swastika and the sacred syllable *om* or *aum*, and the ankh from ancient Egypt.

After a while, the movement appears to have suffered from internal dissension, and its influence dissipated somewhat. The need for guidance became apparent, and after searching for a leader or quasi-messianic figure to take the movement forward, the theosophical leaders came upon a youth, Jiddu Krishnamurti. He was nurtured by the theosophists, and although ultimately he disowned the theosophy movement, his significance in this study of global non-duality is important.

He gave many talks and wrote a number of books and today is considered an authority of high calibre. He stated that as far as his aim was concerned that "I am concerning myself with only one essential thing—to set man free. I desire to free him from all cages, from all fears, and not to found new religious sects, nor to establish new theories and new philosophies."[7] That much is, I suppose, a relief! The teaching contained in mindful philosophy is not new—rather, it could be described as perennial. The need for the taking in hand of the personal small self and its subsumption within the true Self is as old as humanity itself.

Krishnamurti was at pains in his books to emphasise that in order to move away from ego, the "little man within", we must move out of the past and into the present. The ego only thrives because of memories. Without decrying our memories, Krishnamurti advises that the important point is not to identify with them, for that pre-empts our natural ability to engage with what confronts us in the here and now. And what actually confronts us is an unending series of boundaries and limitations if we go down the road of the ego, whereas if we come into the present moment, the ego vanishes, the true Self reigns supreme, and what was formerly seen as limitation, obstacle, or boundary can be accommodated as simply a line drawn as part of a whole. "And in that distance, the division between the seer and the thing seen, in that division the whole conflict of man exists."[8] So Krishnamurti was an exponent of unity philosophy, and through his books was very influential. The manner in which his teachings are disseminated will obviously vary to suit the tastes, culture, and abilities of specific groups, but Krishnamurti was outlining a universal perspective which, for our purposes here, is what is important.

So Krishnamurti eschewed allegiance to any particular religion, philosophy, or grouping. Initially, he was nurtured under the tutelage of the then theosophical leader Annie Besant, but there developed both legal and spiritual problems as a result of which Krishnamurti decided to embark upon his own agenda, unfettered by having to comply with the ideas of others. His fame as a teacher and author took him to engagements with Nehru and Indira Gandhi in India, at the United Nations, with the Dalai Lama, and with associations with distinguished scientists such as David Bohm and Rupert Sheldrake. He outlined three principles:

i) It is essential not to maintain an attitude of sectarianism. One must not be consumed by a partial view, but look holistically. A global stance is required to ensure that ego concerns of a prejudicial nature cannot become dominant.

ii) Environmental matters must receive paramount consideration, because nature is Divine and because human beings are part of the dynamic of nature. This requires appropriate education and an attitude of positivity and reciprocity between peoples.

iii) Spirituality—there needs to be a "religious spirit" to see things from the true perspective and get away from segregation.

The theosophical movement attracted interest from many spiritual authorities. The renowned English author and spiritual teacher Paul Brunton was known as a theosophist. The American author and philosopher Alice Bailey was associated, as was, for a while, Rudolph Steiner, although he ultimately left to start his own movement of anthroposophy that we briefly considered in chapter 4. Krishnamurti was also an influence with the mid-twentieth-century author and philosopher Aldous Huxley. Huxley was a committed spiritual seeker, and ultimately wrote a comprehensive and learned treatise on the subject in his book *The Perennial Philosophy*. So our direction of travel from the mindful philosophical perspective needs to look at what this might mean.

Perennial Philosophy

The title of the present book, at least so far as its content is concerned, could equally have been *Perennial Philosophy*. This title is one that has been appearing from the time of the Neoplatonists and designates the fact that underpinning all the great traditions of the world is a substratum of truth, the realisation of which comprises the human purpose. Marsilio

Ficino, whose letters are for the first time being translated by the School of Economic Science in London, had studied not only Pythagoras and Plato, but also the Hermetic tradition in which was included the myth of the fate of the god Osiris, who was killed and his body dismembered, but ultimately resurrected by Isis (re - membering that which had been dis - membered).

This dying and resurrecting god-man was replicated in Greece by way of Dionysius, and the tradition thence found its way into various pagan teachings, including Attis from Syria, Mithras from Persia (via Rome), and ultimately reappears in Christianity (in particular the Gnostic interpretation thereof). The symbolism is of the annihilation of the small self by way of crucifixion or other means, and the resurrection after three days of the god-man who, as the true immortal supreme Self "ascends into heaven", and to dwell (merge with) the "Father" (the Absolute, Monad, or non-dual essence).

This approach requires acceptance that lying within each and all of us exists that Divine essence awaiting realisation. And it is this line of reasoning that appears in Ficino, and his successors Pico della Mirandola and Agostino Steuco, who uses the term *perenni philosophia* to entitle a book in which is stated that there exists "one principle of all things, of which there has always been one and the same knowledge among all peoples". This notion of universality formed the basis for the perennial philosophy to inform a wide variety of later schools, including what is now called Neo-Advaita, the Transcendentalists, and Unitarians in the United States, and in the process using teachings from Advaita Vedanta, Buddhism, Sufism, and the Baha'i teachings, and of course, Christianity.

St Augustine of Hippo referred to this in a famous quotation referring to the "true religion": "The very thing that is now called the Christian religion was not wanting among the ancients from the beginning of the human race, until Christ came in the flesh, after which the true religion, which had already existed, began to be called 'Christian'."[9]

Sadly, that universal view of human spirituality has been usurped by much of what is now regarded as orthodox Christianity which, it seems, can no longer countenance anything beyond a narrow interpretation on the lines that to give credibility to anything beyond the canonical gospels or biblical texts would be heretical or pagan. But under the auspices of perennial philosophy, it immediately becomes apparent that universal truths are just that.

In point of fact, the great wisdom of paganism, intimately bound up with Gnosticism, actually included the Graeco/Roman traditions inclusive of Socrates/Plato, the Stoics with Epictetus and Marcus Aurelius, and the great Gnostic teachers such as Valentinus, Plutarch, and Basilides. This area has been thoroughly researched by Freke and Gandy in their fascinating book *The Jesus Mysteries*. Some of these teachings were latterly incorporated into Christianity (see chapter 3), but sadly, orthodox or literalist Christianity seems not to accept the bigger view. Neither has it accepted the data from the Nag Hammadi texts, and the profound implications so far as the mystical side of Christianity is concerned, contained therein.

So—what is the bigger view? Aldous Huxley is probably the most articulate of the more recent proponents of the perennial philosophy. In his book of that name one can deduce a number of basic principles, including:

- There exists a "Divine Ground" of all existence. This can be referred to as a spiritual Absolute. This is given various names across human experience, such as the Brahman, the Tao, the Christ within, the Buddha nature, and so on.

- This Divine ground can be directly experienced and realised by the human being.

- The last end of human beings, or the ultimate reason for human existence, is unitive knowledge of the Divine ground.

- This means one has to "die to self". In other words, the small self, little "I", must die so that the being essentially is "born again" as the true Self, big "I", Divine and full of peace and bliss.

- The opportunity to gain "unitive knowledge" will, one way or another, continually be offered until all sentient beings realise who they are, in truth.

At this stage, it might be as well to recapitulate how we commenced this appraisal. In chapter 2, we started by appraising what was meant by the term *non-dual* philosophy. To do this, four precepts were given. They are very similar to what Huxley (with reductions by this author) has outlined above. So we can now see what a powerful thrust of universal timeless philosophy is being promulgated by Huxley and others, all headed straight for us as students in the twenty-first century. Huxley was writing just before the publication and analysis of the Nag Hammadi scrolls (he would, I'm sure, have been delighted to see his teachings so thoroughly and clearly vindicated therein).

And latterly there has been the whole impetus of mindfulness, which in the most practical and holistic manner contains guidance as to how we might take practical steps individually to realise the philosophy teachings, and so convert theory into practice. At this point, perennial philosophy becomes mindful philosophy.

The perennial teachings were in part informed by a number of spiritual teachers from India, or gurus, which is the direction to which we now need to return.

Neo-Advaita and the Teachings of the Gurus

Neo-Advaita is perhaps the most influential and far reaching of the spiritual pathways being availed in the West today. Most of the bestselling authors whose works are now filling the bookshelves in our present-day stores could be described as Neo-Advaitins. It is difficult to overestimate the influence this path has had and is having. One may legitimately enquire as to whether there is any difference between it and what might be called traditional Advaita, and if so, what?

Well, there is some contention here, but that is a road I am not travelling. Either there is non-duality, or there is not. Advaita, as has been amply outlined in chapter 6, is as old as humanity and as new and fresh as a daisy. Of course, any aspirant embarking along that path (or, for that matter, any other spiritual roadmap) will need to practice and be fully committed, and that is the area which I believe has been of concern. But one has to start from somewhere, so using the language and communication methodology of today is to be encouraged and will without doubt be the means whereby many seeking aspirants will be introduced to what arguably is the greatest teaching the world has to offer. It does need to be emphasised that any serious and committed spiritual seeker will need to accommodate such principles in day-to-day living and not just flip through the guidance in the manner of a dilettante. The choice is down to us, but for the purposes of this book Advaita is Advaita, new or old, for ultimately it is all about living inclusively, in the present moment, in the search for Self realisation.

There seem to have been two most commonly encountered streams of Advaita-based teachings coming out of India since the mid twentieth century; one directly from the teachings of Shankara from the line of successive teachers since his time, referred to as Shankaracharyas (*acharya* is a Sanskrit term meaning "teacher", so the word literally means "teachers of the way of Shankara"). The other is the steady stream of Advaita-based teachers emanating from the early-twentieth-century teacher and spiritual guide Ramana Maharshi. In addition to these, there are many individual teachers whose remit seems to have been to engage with the kindling of interest in Eastern mysticism in the West, by offering audience or consultation with individuals or groups. There is a considerable volume of these, well beyond the remit of an introductory book of this type, so we will confine ourselves to briefly considering the two mentioned above.

Looking first at the Shankara tradition directly, it is the intention of the guardians of this "holy tradition", that this tradition should be maintained in an uncontaminated and undiluted state by way of four seats of learning in India—the north, south, east, and west. This tradition is not what is normally referred to as Neo-Advaita, despite the fact that it is very much alive and well today. Each of the four seats should be occupied only by a fully realised man or teacher—someone who has come to "full realisation" or who has realised fully who and what they are and who have been carefully prepared for this high profile and public role, thus providing an appropriate standard of care and protection for the teachings.

This tradition has been of immense and long-lasting benefit to the Western world. The last occupant of the northern seat, Sri Shantananda Saraswati, has been quoted above, and following his copious guidance to the West courtesy of the endeavours of such organisations as the Study Society and the School of Economic Science (both actively and energetically offering courses, teachings, lectures, and publications on the philosophy of non-duality today), was responsible for the promulgation of a particular type of meditation. This is sometimes known as "transcendental meditation", and one of its most well-known exponents is the Maharishi Mahesh Yogi, who was an envoy of that tradition for that purpose.

This type of mantra-based meditation is arguably one of the most beneficial and wide-reaching influences on Western society since the 1960s, and demonstrates quite graphically the commitment of this "holy tradition" to the well-being and spiritual development of the Western world. The influence of this practice is such that vast swathes of the general public took it to their hearts, influenced no doubt in part by the gravitation towards Eastern mysticism of popular rock bands such as the Moody Blues and the Beatles: ("Imagine all the people living for today ... You may say I'm a dreamer, but I'm not the only one. I hope someday you'll join us, and this world will live as one." [John Lennon, *Imagine*]). From the personal perspective, I have practiced this type of meditation for over thirty years and regard it as a fundamental plank of my life. I would recommend it to anyone.

Ramana Maharshi taught that to come to true unity one needs to diligently and persistently enquire "Who am I?" This is known as the *vicara* method. He advises that one needs to "forbid the mind to dwell on (mental obstructions) and to introvert it into the self, and there witness unconcernedly all that happens; there is no other method". With the mind controlled, all else is controlled, and in this way, it may be surrendered and so allow the being to be absorbed in the self. He continues:

> *Distracted as we are by various thoughts, if we could continually contemplate the Self, which is itself God, this single thought would in due course replace all distraction and would itself ultimately vanish; the pure Consciousness that alone finally remains is God. This is liberation. ... Even though the mind wanders restlessly, involved in external matters, and so is forgetful of its own Self, one should remain alert and remember: The body is not I. Who am I? ... "Who am I?" is the only method of putting an end to all misery and ushering in supreme Beatitude. Whatever may be said and however phrased, this is the whole truth in a nutshell.[10]*

One of the first and most influential of Ramana Marhashi's teachings was the English author and mystic Paul Brunton. Brunton produced a number of memorable books, including *A Search in Secret India*, *A Search in Secret Egypt*, and the philosophical treatise "The Inner Reality", a work which outlines non-dual teaching in a lucid and clear manner (referred to in chapter 2). Brunton refers to the *overself* as a means of comprehending the true Self as the Absolute. In a discussion as to what constitutes what is referred to in the Christian tradition as the "kingdom of Heaven", he says that it is a state of being *behind* mind and matter in which one grows and returns, referred to as Spirit, or the overself.

It has no shape or form. It is akin to light, but transcends even that. If we are to go down the road of self-enquiry as recommended by Ramana Maharshi, "You must then no longer look for God as LIGHT, but as YOUR OWN SELF ... You are a Ray of God. To know God is to be God, not to see God. To see implies duality, the relationship of one who sees and that which is seen, but TO BE implies no relationship whatsoever, only the fusion of the Ray with the Sun. This is the highest state of spiritual unity to which you can obtain."[11] He goes on to explain that in addition to our own commitment one also requires "grace", which is something hard to define but universally availed under the appropriate circumstances, for which purpose a teacher is of the greatest benefit. In my experience, the powerful help of a group of fellow travellers under suitable guidance is hugely beneficial. An attitude of humility and mental silence is conducive to receiving fine and subtle teachings of this kind.

From Maharshi Ramana, other teachers such as Papaji, and modern exponents of non-duality such as Mooji, are all part of the plan for our well-being and education in these matters. There are many powerful teachers today. We have already encountered the teachings of the well-known

Advaitin Nisargadatta Maharaj, who died in 1981, but whose publications and teachings based upon enquiry into "Who am I?" and "desirelessness" are becoming increasingly well known.

Deepak Chopra, as an eminent scientist and medical practitioner, writes in an analytical and quasi-scientific manner, espousing Advaita Vedanta–based teachings in a genre which accommodates the rational requirement of the interested reader of the twenty-first century. He produced a concise and practical book known as *Seven Spiritual Laws of Success* which is an ideal introduction to non-dual philosophy with a very Western/scientific approach, and a good prelude to his weightier literature.[12]

And Eckhart Tolle has produced a remarkable range of books which are beautifully and concisely written, offering a lucid insight into what it means to disassociate from identification with the mind and so be really and fully engaged with the present moment. There will be more of this in due course, but suffice to say now that it is the capacity to bring these teachings down to earth, to make them real within the mind of the general broad minded reader, that places writers like Tolle in a unique position of accessibility. Nothing in the output of Tolle and teachers like Timothy Freke and Ken Wilber can be said to do other than to enhance the experience of us all, because they use the language of the vernacular. Communication is essential if the greatest availability of these teachings to the greatest number of would be aspirants, like you and me, is to be achieved.

I referred earlier to the Zen Buddhist master Thich Nhat Hanh and specifically to his holistic manner of putting across mindful or unitive teachings, again in a manner accessible to the general reader. He has the gift of clarity and simplicity—the hallmarks of all great spiritual teachers. His exposition of mindfulness resonates in twenty-first century surroundings which one simply would not have dreamt would be possible a few decades ago. This is all part of the emergence of a new spiritual energy permeating the planet at the dawn of what is being described as a *New Age*—which undeniably it is.

Thich Nhat Hanh is of the Buddhist tradition, not the Neo-Advaita one, but for this purpose this is a semantical differential only—his recommendations are, so far as I can see, identical with those of Indian extraction, and what is today called mindfulness is the practical application of philosophical teachings from many and various sources going back millennia. In fact, the School of Economic Science, a worldwide organisation with its base in London, has been offering courses in what it calls "practical philosophy" ever since the 1950s on precisely these lines, and it continues to do so, as referenced above. For further information, see the notes under chapter 2 at the end of the book.

Finally, and to bring us right up to date, there is the profound and ongoing output of the American thinker and philosopher Ken Wilber. Wilber starts as a transpersonal psychologist, and over a considerable period of time has evolved a theory of "integrational spirituality". He seeks to produce an inclusive, integrationalist theory of everything (he produced a most insightful book thus entitled, amongst many others[13]). His path has been shaped by study of Taoism, Mahayana Buddhism, and Advaita Vedanta. He has had to endure significant personal tragedy. He makes use of the idea of holography, the idea that creation is basically an evolving series of self-contained and discrete yet evolving *holons*.

This theory is not new, deriving from Arthur Koestler and others. There is, for example, a holon comprising subatomic particles. One can envisage this as contained within a discrete bubble. But this bubble, together with a number like it, form another discrete entity, the atom. This new entity, the atom, bands together with other similar groupings to form the molecule. And one can see how there are innumerable discrete bandings, or holons, giving a progression to cells, multicellular substances and so on, to end up with solar systems, galaxies and universes. There is a "holarchy" which defines the relationship between holons at different levels of a particular organisation, and there is the idea of the depth of a holon—its location within the holarchy. So a holon is a whole that is part of other wholes.

These holarchies are what ultimately creates the "kosmos", in which four quadrants can be discerned:

(i) "I", or upper left, the individual consciousness; the interior of individual consciousness;

(ii) "We", lower left, the interior of collective, so communal values, worldliness, cultural settings;

(iii) "It", upper right, exterior of the individual, so brain, body, objectivity, empiricism, scientific data; and

(iv) "Its", lower right, exterior of the collective, nature, social systems, environment, and so on.

The significance of all this, not to mention a range of other integrationist theories such as "spatial dynamics", is simply to ultimately comprehend how integrated everything is. This leads to the questioning of the reality of perceived boundaries. There is another book entitled *No Boundaries*,[14] dealing with our seeming wish to draw up boundary after boundary, which are symbolic of battle lines if we believe them to be real. In the last resort, neither the manifest world nor the boundaries are real.

The ultimate boundary is, of course, that which separates Self from egoic self. R And the need is to see that for what it is, and so attain "unitary consciousness". Unitary consciousness is the ultimate goal, without which we are repatriated back into the world of boundaries, of bondage by time, suffering and mortality. The ultimate reality is devoid of boundaries, and is said to comprise "the simple feeling of being", without form, or any preconceived structure. In espousing the wisdom of Advaita and Mahayana Buddhism, Wilber also makes reference to what he calls "neo-perennialism", to the extent that ultimately reality comprises non-duality—genuinely "no boundary".

The input of Ken Wilber is profound and thought provoking, and a brief work such as this one cannot do justice to his scholarship and depth of understanding. But one can appreciate the direction of travel from statements such as the following extract, discussing what he calls the "transcendent self", the "inward I":

Indeed, what is that? It was not born with your body, nor will it perish upon death.it is without colour, without shape, without form, without size. It sees the sun, clouds, stars and moon, but cannot itself be seen. It hears the birds, the crickets, the singing waterfall, but cannot itself be heard. It grasps the fallen leaf, the crusted rock, the knotted branch, but cannot itself be grasped.

Anytime you identify with a problem, an anxiety, a mental state, a memory, a desire, a bodily sensation or emotion—you are throwing yourself into bondage, limitation, fear, constriction, and ultimately, death. These can all be seen, and thus are not the Seer. On the other hand, to continuously abide as the Seer, the witness, the Self, is to step OUT of them.

This is a simple but arduous practice, yet its results constitute nothing less than liberation in this life, for the transcendent Self is everywhere acknowledged as a ray of the Divine. In principle, your transcendent Self is of one nature with God (however you might wish to conceive it). For it is finally, ultimately, profoundly God alone who looks through your eyes, listens with your ears, and speaks with your tongue.

This then, is the message of Jung: and more, of the saints, sages, and mystics, whether Amerindian, Taoist, Hindu, Buddhist, Islamic or Christian: at the bottom of your soul is the soul of humanity itself, but a divine, transcendent soul, leading from bondage to liberation, from enchantment to awakening, from time to eternity, from death to immortality.

Ken Wilber, No Boundary

CHAPTER 9

THE DATA FROM MODERN SCIENCE

In the history of science, ever since the famous trial of Galileo, it has repeatedly been claimed that scientific truth cannot be reconciled with the religious interpretation of the world. Although I am now convinced that scientific truth is unassailable in its own field, I have never found it possible to dismiss the content of religious thinking as simply part of an outmoded phase in the consciousness of mankind, a part we shall have to give up from now on. Thus in the course of my life I have repeatedly been called to ponder on the relationship of these two regions of thought, for I have never been able to doubt the reality of that to which they point.[1]

Werner Heisenberg (quantum physicist)

I am not a scientist, and have no particular knowledge of matters scientific. This chapter is not a treatise on scientific evidence, theory, or practice. The idea, however, is to see if the leading scientific authorities of the recent past can offer the mindful philosopher any guidance as to what and where, from the scientific perspective, reality might be apprehended. After all, if mindful philosophy is to be accepted as a genuine and substantive approach to life and the living thereof, it needs to appeal universally, including being convincing within a scientific context. There was a time when science and spirituality were not seen as opposites, but complementary. From ancient Greece to Isaac Newton, there was no reason not to admit the deity into the scientific understanding. But with Charles Darwin, whose reverence was for "nature" as opposed to God, there was a splitting away of science from spirituality by way of veering towards a mechanistic materialist approach. To cut a long story short, it is this materialist thinking which now dominates scientific orthodoxy, by which everything in creation is dubbed mechanical, of temporary duration, and ultimately, following the second rule of thermodynamics, is doomed to destruction—including you and me. The universe has no meaning—just a "fortuitous concourse of atoms" (Bertrand Russell). And, if I have understood correctly, this is still the scientific establishment philosophy today.

There are, however, some brave souls whose perspectives, fuelled by free thinking and the true spirit of scientific enquiry, is not hidebound by this "scientific religion". They weigh the evidence, as opposed to hunkering down amidst the strictures of convention, establishment thinking, and emotionally driven prejudice. It is to these teachers and scientific philosophers that we need to turn to if we are to extricate true meaning from the fascinating areas of research which have evolved out of the last hundred years or so. Frankly, the outlook for humanity seems pretty bleak without a full and proper engagement by all of us, including the scientific community, with the make-up of true reality, which of necessity means comprehending and adopting the profound implications of modern quantum mechanics and associated research. As Albert Einstein so graphically explained in 1954:

> *A human being is part of the whole called by us universe, a part limited in time and space. We experience ourselves, our thoughts and feelings as something separate from the rest. A kind of optical delusion of consciousness. This delusion is a kind of prison for us, restricting us to our personal desires and to affection for a few persons nearest to us. Our task must be to free ourselves from the prison by widening our circle of compassion to embrace all living creatures and the whole of nature in its beauty. The true value of a human being is determined by the measure and the sense in which they have obtained liberation from the self. We shall require a substantially new manner of thinking if humanity is to survive.[2]*

Einstein, as is the case of many of the greatest scientists, was deeply spiritual, and his advice here is to get on with it. He is espousing a true non-dual approach, and his advice is to see the limitations of "little I" and move on.

We used a pair of biblical/religious quotations in chapter 6, both purporting to advise that "in the beginning was the word"—very direct and simply expressed data from both the Christian tradition, and also several thousand years earlier from the Vedanta from India, expressing the same thing about the origin of creation. And this is reflected in countless other wisdom traditions, including the Logos from Greece, Plotinus, and the Hermetic school, amongst others. I hope to show below that these statements are reflected in what modern physicists and biologists seem to have been convinced of, namely that in the beginning was the Big Bang and that all that was made is encapsulated in the ever expanding universe, which, by virtue of what is known as the zero-point field (or quantum vacuum field), demonstrates a creation full of creativity and intelligence, response and love, and not the one of materialism or mechanistic reactivity only that has been outlined above.

Holons and Morphic Resonance

Let us take a closer look both at what this means and what might be the implications. In the last chapter, we considered the notion of holons, courtesy of Ken Wilber, who uses Arthur Koestler's nomenclature to illustrate a philosophical point. Now, holons illustrate an order and a direction of travel. As each holarchy evolves, the whole can be seen to be greater than the sum of the parts. For example, in a book like this, each chapter can to some extent be seen to stand up on its own. But put together in a book, it is obvious that they relate to each other in a way that carries much more weight and meaning than is the case individually. And so it is with the paragraphs of which the chapters are contained. Likewise, the sentences that make up the paragraphs, the words that make up the sentences, the letters the words, and so on.

And going the other way, this book will no doubt fall into a niche with other books of similar genre, these books then will form part of a teaching or human outlook, and from that will grow other philosophical groupings and tendencies. All are wholes within wholes. This applies to all the structures of nature, which is alive and not a moribund concept, whether we are dealing with minute entities, such as cellular or atomic structures, or vast ones, such as cosmological or galactic ones. Now the point about this, if we are to believe modern physicists such as Rupert Sheldrake, is that new holons are continuing to evolve and that they have a life of their own, which is capable of reacting to experience, and can seem to transcend our old friends that we looked at in chapter 6, namely time, space, and causation. Sheldrake has evolved a methodology about this, in which he attempts to explain how it can be that ideas and concepts seem to just expand, come to fruition and develop, sometimes on a global basis and within a very short timeframe, with no obvious cause. All that we know is that there seems to be a certain resonance that is in synchronicity with the ethos of the moment. He has coined the term *morphic resonance* to describe these occurrences.

Morphic resonance is described by Sheldrake as a derivative of the holon, or hierarchies thereof, the wholeness of which, in each case, depending upon a sphere of influence, or field. They are vibratory patterns of activity, interacting electromagnetically with the quantum field system it's responsible for. Such "morphogenetic" fields include fields shaping the development of plants, animals, and their instincts and patterns of behaviour, together with social and mental fields. One particular facet is that they are shaped by morphic resonance from previous similar systems, and so exhibit memory. There is no space or time limitation. They operate by imposing patterns upon what are otherwise random events in the systems under their influence.

Full information on all that this comprises may be gained by reference to the books and data issued by Rupert Sheldrake. I have used *The Science Delusion* for this purpose.[3] I would strongly recommend this publication to the scientifically motivated mindful philosopher, where full scientific data and discussion is available, well beyond the scope of this book. Suffice to say that these morphic fields can explain, for example, why and how human ideas and concepts can suddenly explode into activity—their "time is right". The rapid development of steam driven power during the nineteenth century is an example—after this had been pioneered in the United Kingdom. The change in fashionable ideas, such as the present "green" movement which is shaping the opinions of, in particular, the current younger generation, is another case. The sudden expansion of spirituality in the West during the 1960s is another. In fact, Sheldrake makes the case for memory being dependent upon morphic resonance.

This is also something articulated by the well-known physicist David Bohm, who was of the view that the "implicate" or enfolded order, or in non-dual philosophy parlance the "subtle world", exhibited a memory function which enables the emergence of the gross physical world, or the "explicate" or unfolded order. Memories are an important part of these ideas, because provided that there exists some kind of vibratory system with which they can resonate, they can continue as part of collective memory after death of the physical body. Sheldrake explains that one of the more obvious hallmarks of morphic resonance is the observable fact that in both humans and animals, a new fashion, or, in the case of animals a new trick, once learned, can quickly find its way across the globe. Mobile telephone and IT use are probably good examples—the older generation is dumbstruck at the speed and efficacy with which the younger are able to simply close with and adopt the new technology.

Sheldrake has also researched how this works with, for example, the ability of homing pigeons to find their way back to base with no apparent aid, even from out to sea. And there is the case of dogs who seem to sense when their owner is en route home. This all implies some kind of memory, which in turn implies some kind of consciousness or awareness which inhabits and pervades all of the "implicate order" so that it can be made manifest in the "explicate order". And that awareness is universal—there plainly cannot be any notion of division or apportionment of awareness if it can so comprehensively inhabit all the created universe in this way.

Zero-Point Field

We can see the earth set against the background of billions of stars, and galaxies and clusters of galaxies. I had the experience of recognising that it's all connected—that it is not, as we in science tend to believe, a cosmic accident; it's all not that way at all—that the molecules of my body and the molecules of the spacecraft were manufactured in the furnaces of ancient stars billions of years ago. Everything was part of this process that created us, and there is a connection between all of it; and that it's an intelligent universe, not just a piece of inanimate matter floating around.[4]

Thus spoke Edgar Mitchell from within the capsule of Apollo 14. Mitchell was not only a scientist, but also a keen observer of the paranormal, and he used his trip to further his researches into that area. There are a number of similar observations in his book *The Way of the Explorer* (publisher *readhowyouwant.com 2009).*This particular quotation was handed to me as part of a philosophy course I attended. Mitchell resumed his career in physics by way of enquiries into what might explain the seemingly all-pervasive link or connection between everything. This was in the 1970s. Since then, there has been a great deal of research across the scientific community into what might be this connection, or at least what might be the manifestation of such a connection to which good use might one day be put. At this point, the world of quantum physics comes to our aid. Quantum physics is a discipline which has mind-boggling implications, and has turned the scientific world upside down ever since Einstein articulated his theory of relativity. Again, this is not a book for the technically minded, but suffice it to say that it is now commonly accepted that the focus around which materialist philosophy revolves, namely matter, has been proven by scientists themselves to not actually exist at all.

The "connection" spoken of by Mitchell has been associated by him and many others, including one Hal Puthoff, with a field of energy which pervades space and the universe. Following the exploration of Max Planck, Einstein, and others, Puthoff and his colleagues were able to discover, by way of research using vacuum- and gravity-based data, that empty space is not empty, or space. Their computations reveal that the universe comprises a mass of ceaseless energy. This energy is set within light. Particles apparently ebbed and flowed within this mass.

The scientist Heisenberg then discovered that it was simply not possible to discern simultaneously both the location and the velocity of the particle— either one or the other, but not both—something now known as the "uncertainty principle". It transpired that particles were not hard, solid entities, but were the fulcrum of forces, from which their influence thence stretched out into space. Space is thereby charged full of energy—so much so that apparently one single cubic metre contains more energy than is contained within all the matter in the universe as we understand it. This huge field of energy is known as the *zero-point field*.

There are huge implications here, with a vast and, as yet, untapped energy source at hand. Another philosophically significant implication is the fact that if waves of energy integrate all matter in the universe, then this is conducive to the existence of a universal life force, rather as indicated by the notions of prana or chi, from respectively, the Indian and Chinese ancient spiritual traditions, and from Genesis, the suggestion that from light God created matter.

The author and journalist Lynne McTaggart has produced a composite summary of how the evolution of quantum science has evolved in her wonderful book *The Field*, which it would repay the student of these matters to study.[5] The upshot of this is that matter is not inert, but energy—every apparently hard, solid item is simply an accumulation of energy interfacing with the zero-point field.

Another researcher, Fritz Popp, has revealed that subatomic particles are able to cooperate and evolve into a coherent entity. DNA is able to orchestrate and guide the evolution of cellular structures by way of morphic resonance. Popp's experiments included venturing into the fields of health and fitness—light emitted from the eggs of free-range chickens contained more coherent photons than that from battery hens. Healthy food generally could be seen to be so by way of the measurement of biophoton emissions. Human health, treatments such as homeopathy, and even effecting cures for cancer could be measured and enhanced by admitting more light where it was needed.

And the implications of all this? Well, it seems that science is advising us that creation is simply not what it seems. Rather than comprising nothing more than a mechanical automatic and predictable machine, it transpires that it is seen to be cohesive, to contain an intelligence which can discriminate, and to involve meaning and purpose.

Random-Event Generators

Another development took place took place at the University of Princeton, by way of what is known as the Princeton Engineering Anomalies Research Laboratory (PEAR) in the 1990s. This involved the development and, under the most rigorous parameters, the use and experimentation with, machines operated by use of the focus of human attention or consciousness upon a given set of options. They are known as *random-event generators*, or REGs. The results over many years have covered many fields of activity, from simple yes/no-type answers to paranormal data.

There is not the scope in this book to go into details, but this is well documented in the relevant reports and technical literature from PEAR and elsewhere, and from the main researchers (Jann and Dunne)—but it seems beyond dispute that the results achieved are manifestly above "chance" proportion. This has attracted the attention of the US National Research Council. From the perspective of mindful philosophy, the data emanating from these researches is of interest because it appears to be concluding that subjects are able to transcend time—they can inhabit both future and past and so place at some doubt the notion that time is fixed and given—another precept one would think would be more within the province of the oriental mystic than that of the twenty-first century researcher. Nothing, it seems, is sacred; the idea of normal time progression, cause and effect, and of solid objects surrounded by space are to be replaced by an all-pervasive and -encompassing *here* and *now*.

Further researches into dreams illustrate the fact that future and past are all contained in the all-encompassing zero-point field. Time and space create separateness, whereas integration takes place in the present. The physicist Robert Jahn, the REG developer, explains that to remove the notion of time from our consideration of reality is simultaneously to remove our separation. Conversely, to give credence to space and time is to promulgate our sense of separation, and so to create separate objects. In a derivative of this rationale is the whole world of prayer or petition—if simple attention via the REG machines is capable of defining the actuality of what one might refer to as "subtle" (random) energy, then maybe directed attention by way of prayer could do the same?

Certainly the revelations of the US former neurosurgeon Eben Alexander in his book *Proof of Heaven* are most trenchant. Alexander was a typical product of the medico/scientific establishment, highly successful and confident, until he contracted a rare, almost terminal, illness (E. coli bacterial meningitis), which locked him into a coma for seven days. He appeared to be very close to death. He went through a near-death experience (NDE), and upon relating his experiences after his recovery he was at pains to relate that it was the prayers and support from his loved ones that were of most significance to him, whist he was undergoing the NDE. Could this be further data where by courtesy of our understanding of the zero-point field that science has integrated with the "mystical" in yet another area?

Vitalism—The Data from Stem Cell Biology

Another area where contemporary scientific research is furthering the principles of mindful philosophy is that of stem cell research. The internationally acclaimed microbiologist Dr Bruce Lipton undertook researches which led to the establishment of an experimental tissue-transportation system, which ultimately was used to progress the area of human genetic engineering. He discovered that there appeared to be some form of intelligence associated with the outer layer of the cell, which seemed to behave as its mind.

This process had a profound effect upon him, to the extent that he abandoned his former atheistic beliefs in favour of the apparent existence of a Divine principle which his researches were implying. This is fully explained in his book *The Biology of Belief*.[6] His take is that rather than life being controlled by genes, which is the establishment view of genetic scientists, his researches demonstrate that genes are activated or laid to rest by environmental factors operating by way of the cell membrane. So this means that the manner in which we interpret the environment around us is crucial in terms of the effect upon our genes and so upon our life. And one of the most significant factors controlling our environment is the belief system, or perception of reality, that we inhabit. If, therefore, we put into practice the holistic and inclusive approach as described in this book under the term *mindful philosophy*, then under this idea life stands a better chance of being lived under conditions of well-being and good health than would otherwise be the case.

Lipton used the data from this study of epigenetics to demonstrate that by using cell biological mechanisms it was possible to confirm that the physical body was controlled by the mind, and not vice versa. And that this in turn implied the existence of a controlling spiritual entity. These award-winning researches were availed to the public. They also were applied to his own personal biology which he analysed and recorded in the interests of embarking upon a programme of analysis and application to verify how leading edge science can interact with mind/body therapy within a spiritual context—"energy mechanism". This new biology, or "vitalism", makes it quite clear that what is required is a holistic approach to health care, inclusive of spiritual healing.

Sound and Resonance

If modern science is turning our perceptions round to the extent that there is no such thing as matter because it is it is all energy, then of what is this energy constituted? Well, the best answer is that it cannot really be defined or quantified, but by way of waves of energy or light, it can be discerned, or the existence of "something" can thereby be implied. We looked at the ideas of the New Zealand biologist Darryl Reanney above in chapter 7, in that he is of the view that resonance is a kind of recognition, before the waves have been "collapsed" into physical sound. Looking further at his ideas, we need to re-engage with one of the central tenets of quantum theory—namely, that the apparent existence of what is called the "wave/particle" duality is destroyed when consciousness, or attention by way of observation, is applied to the wave, which then "collapses" to a particle. In this way, there has to be consciousness *before* material creation can manifest. There cannot be manifestation of matter without there having been consciousness before.

The implication of this is huge because we are so used to the need to isolate the object of investigation from the observer of that object, thereby creating objectivity—the essential bedrock of scientific appraisal. But with the knowledge that the observer cannot *not* influence the outcome of whatever experiment he is undertaking, what must be the implications for us? Reanney advises that there is only one conclusion—"the world we see is not the world that IS; instead we are confronted with a much more challenging assertion; the world we see is the world we MAKE."

If we are tempted to adopt a dualistic "subject/object" stance, we create problems. We have already seen in our consideration of oriental philosophy that Reanney, together with Timothy Freke in his book *The Mystery Experience*, and the Australian scientist-turned-philosopher Malcolm Hollick in his book *The Science of Oneness* are all agreed that we need to look holistically—the "both/and" approach, not the "either/or", as illustrated by the taijitu symbol. Ken Wilber discusses this, too, using the graphic illustration of drawing a concave line on a drawing board, demonstrating that simultaneously we will have drawn a convex one as well. This is all supportive of the essence of non-duality—that in the last analysis, *all is one*. Reanney goes so far as to tell us that originally, before the "big bang", in other words before there was time, space or causation, all must have been one. After it, he discerns that the nature of atomic structures is that they want to come together—to coalesce, to return to the state of oneness. The tool with which this is accomplished is gravity, the "all-permeating yearning of fragmented energy to again be one". The prism is used as an example of how this works—the wonderful diverse colours are merged together to become a pure white light—the "many become the One", as perceived by Shelley:

The one remains, the many change and pass;

Heaven's light forever shines, Earth's shadows fly;

Life, like a dome of many-coloured glass,

Stains the white radiance of Eternity.

Before we leave Reanney, here is one more of his insights: "All things are One in truth; this means that there can be no separation in truth. This has to be so, for in love which is truth made manifest there is no boundary between being and becoming; they are held in perfect balance as undivided parts of undivided Oneness".

Finally, the interested mindful philosopher should be aware of the existence of an international organisation known as "SAND" – or science and non – duality. This is a valuable asset, as it organises conferences, talks and workshops on this subject, exemplifying the expanding interest in matters spiritual within the scientific community. One of the many well known contributors is Dr. Jude Currivan, who as a physicist/quantum physicist, mathematician, and cosmologist, has researched data from psychical, physical and spiritual phenomena ("multi – dimensional realms") which reveal that the life of the universe is fundamentally interconnected, and rather than comprising a random, separate and materialistic universe, it in fact continues to evolve as a unified entity with a purpose and intention. As she says in one of her addresses made in 2018 in terms reminiscent of Sheldrake and Wilber: *"we are beginning to see the entire universe as a holographically interlinked network of energy and information, organically whole and self referential at all scales of its existence. We, and all things in the universe, are non – locally connected with each other and with all living things in ways that we are unfettered by the hitherto known limits of space and time".*

In summary, there do seem to be many areas of scientific research which are leading us by way of a paradigm shift from the deterministic approaches of the "science religion", in its apparent refusal to countenance the evidence of its own researches. It is high time that in the twenty-first century we evolved out of the embraces of an eighteenth-century physicist (Newton) and a nineteenth-century biologist (Darwin), no matter how forward looking and influential they were in their days.

Mindful philosophy is first and foremost about getting to the truth of what constitutes reality, and I feel that there is a whole world in the scientific field in which the interested layman would do well to show an interest. The important thing here is to put the truth first, irrespective of personal views, opinions, belief systems and ideologies. In the spirit of non-duality, as implied and illustrated by the above researches, we need to re-establish the former unity of science and spirituality/philosophy—another fine example of the "both/and" stance to replace worn-out notions of either/or.

Let us endeavour to summarise a few of the principle ideas of this fairly complex part of this appraisal:

- There is no such thing as matter—only energy.

- There is no such thing as empty space—just continuously moving and all-pervading energy.

- Data from REG machines indicate that time as conventionally understood is an illusion.

- Modern stem cell research indicates the existence of a Divine presence.

- Observation of the smallest particles, electrons (i.e., the application of consciousness by attention) is the only means by which so-called matter can be realised.

- Consciousness therefore pre-exists created matter.

- There can be no phenomenon until it is observed—the "observer effect".

- This rationale is destructive of materialist philosophy because the very thing that sustains materialism—matter—does not, in the last analysis, actually exist.

- There is in truth no separation—"I" am an individualised derivative of a universal consciousness.

As David Bohm said, in terms resonating with Aldous Huxley, "I would suggest that there is some ground, deeper and subtler that either mind or matter, and that they both enfold from this ground, which is the beginning and ending of everything." He went on to explain that

> *the field of the finite is all that we can see, hear, touch, remember, and describe. This field is basically that which is manifest, or*

tangible. The essential quality of the infinite, by contrast, is its subtlety, its intangibility. This quality is conveyed in the word spirit, whose root meaning is "wind", or "breath". This suggests an invisible but persuasive energy, to which the manifest world of the finite responds. This energy, or spirit, infuses all living beings, and without it any organism must fall apart from its constituent elements. That which is truly alive in the living being is this energy of spirit, and this is never born and never dies.[7]

CHAPTER 10

MINDFUL PRACTICE

In this chapter we are going to consider some desirable goals set within the context of mindful practice in order to steer our ship in the direction of what could be described as the aim and purpose of mindful living. These include true and lasting happiness, well-being, and meaning. This chapter is a little longer than the others, but it's sectionalised, and there will be suggestions by way of practical steps we can take within the context of what is today known as mindfulness, or mindful practice. This is the hands-on of mindfulness, and will comprise a number of fundamental areas of human activity such as love, presence, judgement, and reason. The idea is to look at these very basic and fundamental areas from the perspective of non-duality and inclusivity, which are part and parcel of what is now referred to as the mindful way. In the next chapter, we will be looking at various exercises, including the fundamental matter of meditation, these being the means whereby proper implementation of these mindful practices or goals might be realised.

To carry this out, I want first to clarify that mindfulness needs to be considered as a universal approach, not in any way restricted to the

Buddhist or any other spiritual tradition. Nor should it be restricted to the world of therapy, no matter how needy the patient and practitioner, or highly motivated the therapist. If mindfulness is essentially awareness, then it is consciousness. If it is consciousness, then it is indestructible, ever present, and universal. I am talking here not of being aware or conscious *of* something, but just consciousness itself—the simple knowledge that I AM.

This simple knowledge is availed if we can allow the chatterings of the mind to calm down and so to simply rest in our inner being. Then there will be a simple "isness"—no "thing" that can be quantified or defined, but simply the knowledge that "I am". This is a statement of universal truth. It can simply be tested by stating to oneself the opposite—"I am not". A full consideration of that position is likely to reveal that it is deeply inimical and simply not true. After all, who is it who is making the enquiry?

The modern Indian teacher Nisargadatta Maharaj, in answering a question on liberation and consciousness, has stated that we need to withdraw from ideas of the experience so that we can engage with the experiencer, which opens the gate to what he describes as "the only true statement you can make: I AM".[1]

One most useful exercise we can try is simply to keep the feeling of "I am" in mind so that one simply merges in that feeling. Maharaj then advises that with practice we develop what he calls an affection for that state of being and ultimately "stumble on the right balance of attention and affection and your mind will be firmly established in the thought—feeling 'I am'".[2] In fact, it is difficult, in the last resort, to claim with complete certainty that one actually knows anything else.

This position is something that is standard guidance from the great teachers. Socrates, in particular, was known for his ruthless approach to statements of opinion when his students purported to know something, and encouraged his followers to keep investigating by use of what we now call "dialectic"—the search for truth in any given situation. Truth is the goal, not my opinions, belief systems, religious, or political pressures and the like. But the truth that "I am" is given and is the rock on which our edifice of life is then constructed.

Let us take a look again at the definition of mindfulness by the contemporary teacher Jon Kabat-Zinn, possibly the most well-known advocate of modern mindfulness practice, that we briefly encountered in chapter 1. Mindfulness is described as "paying attention in a particular way, on purpose, in the present moment, non-judgementally". There are many definitions of mindfulness, but this one is succinct and all-embracing. It covers many of the basic constituent parts of mindful practice, and emphasises that there needs to be deliberate engagement and practice—"on purpose".

Elsewhere he clarifies that, irrespective of the myriad scientific and medical testings and research projects which confirm the efficacy of mindful practice, that there does need to be committed practice into the long term as a commitment to oneself which "requires a degree of stick-to-it-ness and discipline, while at the same time, being playful and bringing each moment, as best you can, a certain ease and lightness of touch—a gesture of kindness and self-compassion really".[3]

Now anything worthwhile in life needs practice and commitment. The subject matter that we are dealing with here could not be more life changing and life enhancing. So it needs to be taken on board and practiced in the manner of committed application. And, yes, that needs a certain time commitment. This will probably mean seeking and implementing guidance from a teacher, ideally within a group structure or possibly on line. Regular meditation will be needed—this is a big subject which I will consider later, but for the moment the point is that the would-be student of mindful philosophy should not be under any illusions as to the level of commitment needed. That said, day-to-day life will continue very much as it does now or as one wants it to. And the results in terms of well-being and happiness could not be higher.

There are three aspects to mindful practice that are referred to in the quotation. They are attention, presence, and judgement. All are essentially aspects of the same thing, but it would be helpful to take a look at them from the philosophical perspective. By using this process, we will come to a deeper understanding of what is being suggested. Other aspects of mindful practice will be considered thereafter:

Attention

The use and direction of attention is key to the practice of mindful philosophy. Without the proper use and harnessing of attention, there cannot be progress in the direction of wisdom as we have defined it in chapter 1, or of mindful practice. We will all recognise the difference between, say, the attentive receptionist who listens and engages with the would-be patient or client, as opposed to the dismissive inattentive operative, whose attention is plainly not on your needs but upon her/his concerns, resulting in a feeling of neglect or inadequate concern. This is an example of how we have the ability as human beings to direct and focus the attention.

What actually is it that is being focussed or directed? The answer has to be consciousness or awareness. Attention is focussed consciousness or awareness. That focussing can either be very precise, or it can be the opposite—open and unfocussed. It can be focussed in such a way that one is in control of the telescope, as it were, so that the attention can be directed, adjusted, or withdrawn as the need arises. Alternatively, the focussing can seem to be very driven, devoid of control, or all-consuming, as if the telescope mechanism has jammed. These two states can be described as attention under control, or attention captured. The former is a state of freedom yet concentration, whereas the latter is a state of bondage. The former can lead us to higher or enhanced states of awareness, whereas the latter can lead to the development of negative feelings or loss of awareness.

We can look at this process rather more clearly with the aid of a simple diagram:

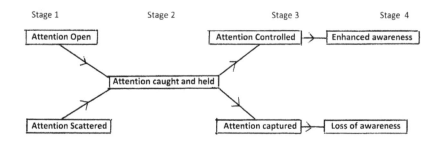

Diagram of States of Attention

This diagram illustrates four options so far as attention is concerned. It outlines four phases or stages through which we have the potential to encounter. The first stage is preliminary. The idea of attention open indicates a free unbound and receptive state. The idea of attention scattered is also unbound, but in a less helpful manner in that one is not really present, perhaps somewhat absent-minded, with the attention jumping around from one topic to another, diffused with no repose.

Ultimately, however, something attracts the attention—phase two, in which there is a moment of choice. This is the critical time, and it may not be easy to spot this choice. The choice will either be made from presence, in true awareness, or can revert to scattered attention or worse, to its being captivated by the world of mental angst or all-consuming imaginings.

Inevitably, the process leads inexorably into the choices outlined in stage three. One may consider that there is not a lot of difference between the states of attention controlled and attention captured. The truth is that there is all the difference in the world. The former state is one where attention is directed upon the object, yet retaining enough awareness so that a change in direction can be embarked upon if needed. Under control, attention is a most potent force, and there are many instances in which the sages and teachers of spirituality have referred to it. In this manner, all one's faculties are made available, and the power of attention stands revealed as probably the most potent and effective power a human being possesses.

This was a favourite topic of the Advaita teacher Vivekananda, who we came across in chapter 7. He wrote a booklet on the subject called *Work and Its Secret*, in which one finds the following which relates to the importance of the means as well as the end:

> *One of the greatest lessons I have learnt in my life is to pay as much attention to the means of work as to its end ... Proper attention to the finishing, strengthening of the means is what we need. With the means all right, the end must come.*[4]

Attention captured is a sorry state indeed, in that rather than the enhanced awareness which is derived from attention under control, there is simply a stage of bondage in which the attention is stuck with some idea, some thought, some emotion or some imagining. This might be some bad news brought by the postman, some emotional loss such as grief, some financial cataclysm, or, indeed, the opposite—a fortune won. All such things can usurp our conscious minds, bringing them into a state of immobility and bondage. Stage four from this perspective is, therefore, a loss of awareness.

To practice in a mindful manner means to maximise awareness, and this means using the great and wonderful powerhouse we call *mind* to its fullest potential, and not allowing it to become contaminated with out-of-control thought processes. One of the great benefits of developing the techniques of mindful philosophy is that it can lead us not only to the ability to use and control the mental world, but will shed light upon the great questions and concerns of philosophy as to what, in truth, "I am". After all, if we discover through our own efforts and application that this "monkey mind" is capable of being regulated, then who, or what, is doing the regulating?

Presence

To occupy the present moment, or to live in the *now*, is seen as the essence of mindful living. This is indeed a most desirable goal, but it seems that in the culture of today, ruled as it is by pressure to indulge in sensory gratifications of every kind, such a goal is difficult to realise. The teacher Alan Watts, in one of his addresses, is quoted below, succinctly outlining the difficulty:

> *We are living in a culture entirely hypnotised by the illusion of time, in which the so-called present moment is felt as nothing but an infinitesimal hairline between a causative past and an absorbingly important future. We have no present. Our consciousness is almost completely preoccupied with memory and expectation. We do not realise that there never was, nor will be any other experience other than present experience. We are therefore out of touch with reality.*

The idea of presence is very closely associated with that of attention, and in essence can be seen as the same thing approached from a slightly different standpoint. The present moment is all that we have. We don't have anything else. There is a famous anonymous saying that "the past is history, the future is a mystery, but the present is a gift, which is why it's called the present". If we are truly present, it will be obvious and self-evident that the present moment is a gift. This gift is the "reality" that Alan Watts is referring to.

If the present moment comprises reality, then what of the other two time frames of past and future? Well, despite the apparent reality of them both, they are both illusory. The only reality is *now*—the present moment. It is the case that it is never *not* now. This is a philosophic reality which in the Christian tradition is referred to as the *nunc fluens* or the *nunc stans*. This approach outlines the apparent paradox of the momentary nature of "now" being sandwiched as a slither of filling between the enormous hunks of bread, each side of which comprise past and present (*nunc fluens*) or the true reality that "now" is timeless, universal, and limitless (*nunc stans*), and which is, therefore, imbued with the essence of the Divine. The former is transient and ephemeral, and the latter is essentially the eternal and so is Divine. The sixth-century Roman Neoplatonist philosopher Boethius, in his book *The Consolation of Philosophy*, stated that "the now that passes (*nunc fluens*) produces time; the now that remains (*nunc stans*) produces eternity."

It is worthwhile reflecting at this point that this capacity for us to realise presence, to realise the true potential of the present moment, referred to by Eckhart Tolle in his bestselling book of that name as *The Power of Now*, is the realisation of the Divine essence which is described in these pages as big I. The method is simple, basically comprising the disassociation of one's identity with the mind and its contents, which thereby can form the subject of detached observation. Any unwelcome power over one's well-being, such as stress or anger, will become dissipated if we can but sever our identity from it by the simple process of observation or just witnessing what is going on.

And that is the true meaning of mindfulness—to realise beyond doubt and in practice who and what I am by becoming present. Can it really be that simple? And is that really all there is to it? Well, yes! But because it is simple, that does not make it easy, and the work of the mindful philosopher and spiritual seeker cannot be said to be a quick fix or a shoo-in to realisation.

What is needed is good company, true teaching, spiritual knowledge, and committed practice, and conducive friendship to help us on our way.

Let us consider the implications of the past/present/future discussion. Dealing first with the past, it is self-evident that by "living in the past" one becomes prey to all sorts of undesirable emotions. Yes, we can and must learn the lessons of the past, but that learning process itself does not take place in the past, but in the now. If we occupy a life in the past, possibly caused by seething resentment, anger or the like, we can become pretty dysfunctional human beings pretty quickly. How many stories are there about, for example, resentment over the contents of a will, leading to a permanent state of jealousy, angst, and tension? And anger over a failed relationship or ruined business transaction? As soon as one realises that these situations have been and gone, and so let go of, then equanimity can return as we re-enter the present moment.

What of the future? Well, it is one thing to make plans and prepare for the future in the now, but quite another to worry incessantly about it. Worry is not conducive to living in the now. Proper preparation however is a function of the present moment. With the attention under control, issues needing our involvement, even if relating to preparing for a future event, can be dealt with devoid of emotional stresses and pressures, cleanly and clearly in the present moment. Going back to Plato and his assertion that the mind, if under control, makes a wonderful servant, but if not, can quickly become a tyrannical master, it is perhaps in worrying about the future where this becomes most obvious. It is the case that incessant worries can usurp our sense of well-being more speedily and effectively than anything else if that is how we operate.

To return to the present and remove our captivity by way of the worries and fears for the future and the resentments and anger deriving from the past, what is needed is the capacity to place both under observation. There does need to be a certain detachment if there is to be any genuine observation. Once placed in context under the gaze of observation, one can allow reason to be activated. Once reason has been allowed to function, a sense of proportion can be established. At that stage one can view things exactly as they are, unadorned by the creatures of the mind which hitherto have played havoc with our state of being. Ideas in the mind characterised by phrases such as "What if ..." or "If only ..." and the like are seen to be the useless and unhelpful adjuncts of little I, the ego, that they are as we become more conscious or aware of how the mind is behaving. Big I has been referred to as the observer, or simply as the witness, and when this is in place the real quality of timelessness and contentment that comprises Presence can be experienced.

Non-Judgement

At first sight, this might seem a strange goal for the mindful aspirant. Surely, we need to form judgements all the time? Surely, we depend upon making reasoned analysis to give effect to our decision taking processes? And does not this power of reason, beyond everything else, mark us out as evolved species when compared to all other sentient beings? That which is referred to by Shakespeare (Hamlet, Act 4 Scene iv) as so precious that it could "fust in us unused" if we do not look after it? The answer to all of that is yes. But that is not what is being referred to in this dynamic.

There is a huge difference between exercising reasoned judgement to appraise a situation in life, and approaching that same situation and investing in it an emotional overlay which transforms judgement to what might be called judgementalism. If one is being judgemental, one is being consumed by personal preferences, tastes, opinions, and the like, with the consequence that we incorporate in our speech an emotional content well beyond the simple appraisal of the data which is the characteristic of true judgement.

This leads to the overuse of adjectives such as "good" and "bad", and to stereotypes and distorted representation. In short, we become opinionated. In such a state the natural power of love is blocked, and the ability to rely upon the light of reason is thwarted. Here is a tale I came across, which, I believe, emanated from the financial crash of 2008, about a man who to his friends and colleagues seemed to be permanently at ease and of well-being, so much so that he never stopped smiling:

There was once a man who was always smiling. However, there came a time when he was dismissed from his job. "How sad, that's bad" said his friends. "yes, it is." said the man.

Shortly after he was offered another job at a higher salary. "That's good," said his friends. "Yes, it is," said the smiling man. But the next day he had a run in with the new boss. "Oh that's bad—to have a row with a new boss so quickly" commented the friends. "Yes, it is" said he. But shortly after the new boss complimented him upon the frankness and honesty of his views and after a short while a pay rise accrued. His friends said, "Well, that's good. Well done." And he said, "Yes, it is."

Time passed by and the smiling man had a severe car accident, and was hospitalised for some weeks "What bad luck." said the friends. "yes, it is." said the smiling man. After a month or so a large cheque for compensation came through the post. The friends were astonished: "Wow. That's so good." they said. "yes, it is." said the smiling man.

The smiling man invested the money in the money market. But along came the financial crash and he lost heavily. "That's just so bad." commented the friends. "yes, it is." said the smiling man. And to make matters worse, he was dismissed from his job. "Well, such bad luck." commented his now erstwhile companions. "Yes, it is." replied the smiling man, still smiling.

> *This time however the conversation ran on: "How come you are still able, after all this adversity when things are so bad, to keep on smiling?" enquired the friends. "Well, I don't see anything bad," said the smiling man. But the friends countered, "But whenever we say something is bad or good you always agree with us saying, 'Yes, it is." "No, I'm not agreeing with you," replied the smiling man. "When I say, 'Yes, it is,' that is simply a matter of acceptance. In my opinion there is neither good nor bad. I just accept things as they are presented. I am quite free from having to make a judgement. And because I just accept things without any need to form a judgement, why should I not at all times retain my smile?"[5]*

The moral to the tale is that if we embark upon the road to judgementalism, we have taken ourselves out of the reality of the situation, and out of the present moment. We are not seeing the actuality. All we are seeing is *our view* of the actuality. So we find ourselves unable to accept what we see, and so lock ourselves up within a prison of bondage and pain. Judgementalism is of the ego, or little I, and in that state of being we will find that harmonious emotions such as love are blocked out of our experience. Whereas proper reasoned judgement is of the true Self, and is conducive to freedom and, because it of necessity involves surrender and acceptance of the situation, it allows our natural love to flow. So one can, in effect, exchange love for this type of judgementalism.

If not, there is the risk that we become as we judge. As Jesus so succinctly put it: "Judge not lest you be judged." Or Shakespeare in Hamlet: "There is neither good nor bad, but thinking makes it so." This is a perceptive remark because it reminds us that it is the unruly and ill-disciplined mind, agent for the ego when not in control, and which is primarily driven by fear, which wants at all times to comment, to judge, to claim and to form attachments. This is how the ego deals with its ongoing and irreconcilable fear of annihilation.

It is as if there is a parrot perched upon one's shoulder giving an unceasing running commentary upon "my life", issuing a plethora of words about every "this or that" which crosses our life journey. By using mindful techniques such as placing the movements of the mind under observation using the exercises we will consider in the next chapter we can make an exit from this situation and use the mind for its rightful purpose, allowing true reason and discrimination to take place. Here is a quotation from *The Power of Now,* when dealing with a query or concern that "the present moment is sometimes unacceptable, unpleasant or awful, Tolle advises:

> *It is as it is. Observe how the mind labels it and how this labelling process, this continuous sitting in judgement, creates pain and unhappiness. By watching the mechanics of the mind, you step out of its resistance patterns, and you can then ALLOW THE PRESENT MOMENT TO BE. This will give you a taste of inner freedom from external conditions, the state of true inner peace.*

Then see what happens, and take action if necessary or possible. Accept—then act. Whatever the present moment contains, accept it as if you had chosen it. Always work with it, not against it. Make it your friend and ally, not your enemy. This will miraculously change your whole life.[6]

Finally, one can see that the same dynamics apply in the macrocosm as in the microcosm. Just as we as individual human beings can become ego obsessed, mind driven, and so deprived of our freedom by rigid ideas and belief systems, leading to fear of the future and anger for the past, so can families, groups, and nation states. One can see, for example, that when centuries of entrenched opinion and bigotry are set aside, such as in Northern Ireland in the 1990s, rapid and substantial progress ensues as the perception was realised that these divisions could be perceived as ephemeral. It was a little like a hot knife cutting through butter. Sadly, there are still instances such as the Middle East where the ego mind reigns supreme, and unless and until the act of surrendering such belief systems and habitual reactions takes place there can be little likelihood of an end to the inevitable suffering that ensues.

States of Awareness

We can now move on to consider further areas of mindful practice. If we are to engage with anything in life, there does have to be a certain application of consciousness, or awareness. Without that, life becomes pretty meaningless. It seems that the amount of awareness manifesting is very variable. Now that implies that there are stages, or graduations, in the amount of awareness, or consciousness (for this purpose, I am using the words awareness and consciousness synonymously), which are available. In fact, there is never any shortage of consciousness, and we are told that everything is imbued with it, as creation is made in the image of the creator. Most spiritual traditions would agree that the immanent creator is contained in all creation, from a lump of rock upwards. It is simply that the amount of consciousness made manifest varies. And so there are graduations in the amount of consciousness manifesting via the evolution of created matter, from the mineral kingdom, to the vegetable kingdom, the animal kingdom, human beings, and beyond. As in each so-called kingdom, so within each constituent part. Thus, we find that each one of us at different times and circumstances exhibits differing levels of consciousness or awareness. Or mindfulness.

I believe that five of these can fairly readily be appreciated—sleep, dream state, autopilot state, awakened state, and state of being fully awake, or higher knowledge. We had a brief encounter with these in chapter 5, but now is the time to consider the implications. Let us take a brief look at them:

i) Sleep. There are various levels of sleep. The deepest sleep is a blissful state, and not much can be said about it, other than the fact that having received it, one is fully rested and the after effect can be very pronounced and most beneficial. There is only minimal awareness—not quite zero as otherwise one wonders whether the being could otherwise have the capacity ever to be aroused from sleep. And one hears tales of the mother being able to be aware of the distress of the young child even in the depths of the deepest sleep.

ii) Dream State. This is very familiar to most human beings, but does tend to get rather dismissed—"only a dream". Dreams can be sweet dreams, or nightmares, and when being experienced are very real indeed. Indeed, they can be most instructive, not only from the perspective of what they might mean or portend (not an area for this book and requiring specific expertise), but as an indicator as to what is, or is not, real. The writer has had the experience of coming out of a dream and entering so-called reality, dozing off again to re-enter the same dream, and awakening for the second time. This provoked some internal considerations, as this seemed to constitute two completely different, but equally valid, states of reality. Alternatively, and this is the important point, neither were ultimately real, but "I", as observer of both, and common to both, was actually and indisputably real. "I" was simply the witness of two independent and seemingly unrelated states of awareness.

iii) Autopilot state. This seems to be a condition in which many of us spend the vast majority of our time. It is a state of which appears superficially to be awake, but when analysed is only partially awake. How many times does one get up in the morning, perform one's ablutions, eat breakfast, go about one's duties, maybe travel in the car, meet up with colleagues or family members and the like, all in a state of semi-wakefulness? We are not really there. We seem to be operating via a kind of autopilot. There is but minimal awareness of what we are doing, where we are doing it, who with, and why. This wonderful and most beautiful creation which we inhabit simply passes us by—it's almost as if it doesn't really exist. And so we run the danger that life starts to lose meaning for us. Why? Because we have entered the land of daydreams. The mind is consumed with worries, fears, regrets, anticipations, what-ifs and if-onlys and oughts and shoulds, and so one's centre of being is completely hijacked from the present moment and is forcibly removed to the land of make-believe, or mental construct, which invariably takes place away from the present, in the past or the future—the land of "Nod". And this is the twenty-first-century dilemma—how to square the circle of awareness, and it is to meet this need that the mindfulness programmes are devised. The natural derivative of this, called mindful philosophy in this book, is there to replace our consciousness back to where it needs to be—centred in the here and now, in the "land of the living".

iv) Waking state. The problem is that if we find that we have gone down the road of autopilot, how do we get out of it, and what do we find when we do? Well, the answer is to come to our senses—literally. The only place we can use our five senses of tasting, scenting, touching, seeing, and hearing is now. And once we engage with the objects of sense, all around us the world becomes an entirely different place. It is one thing to walk down a street, head bowed, utterly engrossed in "mind stuff" to the extent that we have not a clue where we are, what we are passing by, and only just avoiding knocking down other pedestrians, when compared to walking the same street fully conscious and alive. By resting in the now, we find our senses are alert, that as a result the world is a sparkling wondrous place, and realising how privileged we are to be so fortunate as to be involved with it. We see the shops and their contents. We notice the people. We sense the weather, view the clouds and sky. We hear sounds—vehicles, chattering people, babies, footsteps. All is vibrant and alive. And this panoply is ever available, all the time—and all we have to do is to be there and enjoy it. What's not to like? To help us with this, we need memory to operate so that the mind can be used as appropriate and so letting the senses play. The techniques of mindfulness and mindful philosophy are the means whereby teachers of all persuasions have invited us to partake of the world we inhabit in the most natural manner possible, leaving behind habit-forming ideas, attachments and negative emotions so that we actually engage with what is right in front of us—"whatever is in front of you is your teacher".

v) Full wakefulness and higher knowledge. There is yet one further state, if state it be, that we can consider. This is the perfect state of true being, of gnosis, of unity and realisation, and so can be said to illustrate what it must be like to be fully awake. We saw in chapter 6 that when queried by his followers as to truly what he was, the Buddha answered that "I am awake". What might this full wakefulness mean? Well, I believe that essentially it means living in complete unity. We see no separation. There is no sense of inadequacy, loss or deprivation. We will have entered the land of the mystics, of those who are fully Self-realised. The fact that we do not ostensibly meet thousands of such people every day in this blissful unitive state does in no way invalidate their pre-eminent position in terms of human evolution. A condition of pure bliss is not something that most of us can readily comprehend or accept as part of normal living, but I believe most of us at some stage in our lives, even way back as a young child, will have experienced it. The mystics need to be relied upon for further elucidation—ordinary words on the printed page do not have the capacity to enlarge upon this supremely important part of our make-ups. Let's listen to the seventeenth-century English priest and mystic Thomas Traherne, who, in extolling the virtues of the creator of humanity, exclaims in one of his "centuries of meditations":

You never enjoy the world alright, till the sea itself floweth in your veins, till you are clothed with the heavens, and crowned with the stars: and perceive yourself to be the sole heir of the whole world, and more than so, because men are in it who are every one sole heirs as well as you. Till you can sing and rejoice and delight in God, as misers do in gold, and Kings in sceptres, you never enjoy the world.

Such exultation could not emanate from a man who is not familiar with true and full awareness, bathed in unity ("every one sole heirs as well as you"). One wonders what kind of a life Traherne led, and what kind of a character he was. Other examples would include another poet/mystic, William Blake, who famously wrote, "To see the world in a grain of sand / And heaven in a wild flower / Hold infinity in the palm of your hand / And eternity in an hour".

Of necessity I have quoted from accomplished poets and mystics, but this does not negate a most important, and indeed fundamental, point. This experience of unity is not the sole province of the poets, mystics, or those educated in such matters. The truth is that unitive experience lies within the potential of us all. It is our birthright as human beings to experience true bliss. And that, of course, is the whole point of mindful philosophic enquiry, and of spiritual study as a whole—as has been said, to realise the truth of who and what we are.

Desirelessness

The concept of living in a condition totally free from desires, or their equal and opposites, aversions, is another way we can approach mindful living. The easiest way of approaching this is possibly to use the imagination. So I am now going to invite you, the reader, to put this book down after you have digested the next few words, and simply reflect upon this.

Imagine that you are utterly content. There is no notion of any lack. So there is no movement in the mind to require things to be any other than precisely as they are. There is complete equanimity. You feel no lack, no desire for anything at all – a state of pure desirelessness. It is not that you've suddenly acquired something, or got rid of something that's been troubling you. It's a simple realisation that all is as it should be—as Julian of Norwich famously predicted: "And all shall be well, and all shall be well, and all manner of things shall be well." Now what would your life be like if it simply contained nothing but this quiet acceptance in a state of what one might call desirelessness, even if just on a momentary basis?

———————

Let us apply reason to this situation. We can perceive that the mental movements we call desire and aversion are the principle methodology used by the ego, little I, or ahankara, to use the Vedic phraseology, to

235

discommode us, to railroad us from our sense of well-being and induce a feeling of stress, or distress. This takes place, to varying degrees, day in, day out, perhaps several times in the space of an hour. We find ourselves kicked around like a football, unpredictably, and without any seeming control. But we have been told by the wise that that is not how life has to be, and judging by the numerous examples from the wise, both present and past, which have been put forward in this book, it appears that we do have the means whereby this can be governed.

In chapter 2, we considered the three basic component parts of our intrinsic nature, these being being/truth, consciousness/awareness, and bliss/true happiness. Desirelessness is basically the last mentioned—to be fully content and full of well-being without any perceived lack is true happiness. So how do we get to that highly desirable state? Well, I think we need to look a little more closely at the idea of true happiness, and then consider how this might be availed. This is something we touched on both in chapter 2, as it lies within the fourth precept of mindful philosophy as comprising the inevitable outcome of such teaching, and when we were looking at Buddhism in chapter 5. Happiness is the motivating factor for all human activity. We embark upon a course of action, or make a decision, on the assumption, explicit or not, that that direction of travel will increase the sum of my happiness. This is so even if we believe in the short term pain might need to be experienced so that the seed corn of future happiness will be garnered.

But analysis of this soon reveals that there are various types of happiness. There is the simple acquisition of pleasure. The more pleasure I get, the happier I am. This is a commonly held belief, upon which countless TV commercials are based. The only problem is that it is all too readily accompanied by its equal and opposite entity—pain. If I can't get the said provider of pleasure, pain is experienced. So this rather ephemeral state is not to be relied upon, and certainly does not exemplify the blissful state described by the wise. So maybe there's something else.

There are many options. "I'll be happy when …". We defer our happiness, happiness occurring when I retire, when the mortgage is paid off, when I find a partner, when I've finished my project, when I go on holiday, and so on. But is this true? What if these desirable goal get deferred, or even cancelled? The inevitable result is that we experience the opposite of happiness, namely misery. So these potential states of happiness are desire-driven, and are not therefore the state of desirelessness that true mindful living exemplifies. They have their inevitable opposites.

But there is another option. True happiness is not born of desire at all. And it doesn't happen sometime off in the future; it happens right *now*. Conventional happiness is subject dependent. It is dependent upon a thing. True happiness, as we discovered in chapter 5, is Self-dependent. It is dependent upon no thing. We will all have experienced moments of pure uplift and well-being, possibly as young children, when for no explicable reason the world seemed a wonderful and blissful place. Would that we could revert to and inhabit such a place all the time. That is the happiness of the self—big I, as exemplified by the likes of Thomas Traherne, of Rumi, Shankara, and so many others.

Well, according to the wise, we can all realise this state. It is not so much a case of "what can I get to be happy?" as what one has to leave behind, or surrender, to be happy. The light of true happiness is always shining because it is our deep and intrinsic nature. However, the layers of dust and debris concealing this light need to be removed. The question is how this might be undertaken.

There are two words which might help us to see how this can be achieved—detachment and surrender. Desirelessness implies a detachment from the object of desire, and then the desire can be surrendered—it no longer has any power over us. This is something about which we probably have more knowledge than we think. As parents, or maybe in a position of responsibility, we find ourselves having to surrender our desire for pleasure of one sort or another all the time, do we not? Getting up at horrendously early hours, forgoing a lie in in bed, embarking upon all sorts of activities for the benefit of children are part of the normality of life. If we accept these apparent limitations without a grumble and in good grace they are not really limitations at all. That is the hallmark of true surrender—anything and everything we have a desire for can probably form the subject of surrender should the need arise. It is a case of the extent to which we are attached to the object of desire. Sever the attachment and one severs the desire. That is the way to true equanimity and a truly happy existence. To get to that state, that we can see the attachment and thereby realise the ability to surrender it, requires the capacity for detachment. And this is where the spirituality which comprises the essence of us all comes in. Because for there to be detachment, one has first to identify the object from which one needs to be detached—in other words to place it under observation. Now we have seen that to observe anything we must be present and "in the now".

The practice of mindfulness is the key here—the need for attention and presence that we described above will bring to bear upon the situation before us and strengthen our capacity to look properly and fully at whatever issue is binding us to it, so that the desire for it can be recognised for what it is and let go of. So the practice of mindful philosophy can be seen to be very practical and grounded. To be happy means to be non-attached to the proliferations of creation. What it does *not* mean is not to enjoy them. This is beautifully captured in the opening words of the "Isa Upanishad" in which is stated:

"Whatever lives is full of the Lord. Claim nothing, enjoy, do not covet his property". There is no better advice than this towards the desireless state, blissful, peaceful, and full of well-being.

Love

There is one final area I want to consider from the perspective of non-dual mindful philosophic enquiry, and it is the subject of love. The spiritual guide Sri Shantananda Saraswati has referred to love as the "the natural in-between". It is, therefore, a state of being, and can always be availed because it lies within us all. When one is truly present, one can feel a depth of being within which is known to be replicated in every other human being, and in every other sentient being from which there is no separation. Love is inclusive and not exclusive. When love is present, there is no disquiet in the mind, and everything seems so much simpler than when the lack of love creates division, separation and desires of one sort or another.

Love in its pure and uncontaminated form is the natural way to live. The mindful philosopher, being present and attentive, will place pure love as the most important part of life. He or she will be particularly concerned not to allow that purity to become in any way contaminated. To explain, perhaps reference to the Vedic teachings of the gunas we considered in chapter 6 might help. The three gunas, or creative energies, were given as sattva (purity, light, stillness, peace); rajas (motivation, creativity, energy, forcefulness and if in excess leading to stress, angst and loss of stillness); and tamas (inertia, destruction, holding the form of things but if to excess leading to wilfulness, loss of reason and dullness).

Where love is concerned, under sattva it will be guided under wisdom, and will manifest in goodness and natural goodwill and kindness. Love is unconditional. When under dominance of rajas, love can become subject to attachment, and is conditional, rather as described above under desirelessness when succumbing to desires. This can create identifications, and one can the get embroiled with considerations of me, my, or mine, with the inevitable end result of conflict. And when we have love under the spell of tamas, it becomes deluded. In this way there is loss of reason and what would normally be considered true or appropriate becomes the opposite, and vice versa. This manifests in what we would typically consider to be evil, or deluded living.

It is noticeable that under conditions of pure love this state allows reason to function in a steady and unhindered state, whereas under conditions of delusion or contamination reason is either thwarted or completely unavailed. Reason and love are not normally considered as adjuncts to each other, but they are. There is an old adage about the potter's wheel—it is said that to produce a shapely and beautiful pot one needs two hands. There is the hand of reason to hold the clay in position and keep it steady, and the hand of love, to mould the clay into beautiful and fine shapes. This is another example of non-duality—of not *either* love *or* reason, but *both/and* love and reason.

241

To end this section let us take a look at sonnet 116 of Shakespeare, which refers to the constancy and power of true love:

> *Let me not to the marriage of true minds*
>
> *Admit impediments. Love is not love*
>
> *Which alters when it alteration finds,*
>
> *Or bends with the remover to remove:*
>
> *O no! it is an ever-fixed mark*
>
> *That looks on tempests and is never shaken;*
>
> *It is the star to every wand'ring bark,*
>
> *Whose worth's unknown, although his height be taken.*
>
> *Love's not Time's fool, though rosy lips and cheeks*
>
> *Within his bending sickle's compass come;*
>
> *Love alters not with his brief hours and weeks,*
>
> *But bears it out even to the edge of doom.*
>
> *If this be error, and upon me prov'd,*
>
> *I never writ, nor no man ever lov'd.*

CHAPTER 11

WHERE DO WE GO FROM HERE? MEDITATION AND OTHER PRACTICES

Once upon a time, or rather, at the birth of time, when the Gods were so new that they had no names, and Man was still damp from the clay of the pit whence he had been digged, Man claimed that he, too, was in some sort a God.

The Gods weighed his evidence, and decided that Man's claim was good.

Having conceded Mans claim, the legend goes that they came by stealth and stole away this Godhead, with the intent to hide it where Man should never find it again. But this was not so easy. If they hid it anywhere on Earth the Gods foresaw that Man would leave no stone unturned until he had recovered it. If they concealed it among themselves they feared Man might batter his way up even to the skies.

And while they were all thus at a stand, the wisest of the Gods said: "I know, give it to me." He closed his hand upon the tiny unstable light of Man's stolen Godhead, and when the great hand opened again, the light was gone.

243

"All is well. I have hidden it where Man will never dream of looking for it. I have hidden it inside Man himself."

Rudyard Kipling, *"The Thing Hid inside a Man"*[1]

We have considered what the idea of mindful philosophy means by looking at the component parts of what is today referred to as mindfulness, and we've placed this in the context of man's greatest search, which is to discover the truth about himself—who and what he truly is.

We have seen that this consideration of necessity comprises a state, if state it be, of non-duality; that a woman or man is, when all is said and done, a Divine being, not different or separate from the single non-dual entity which is the substratum of existence, variously referred to as God, Allah, the Brahman/Atman, one's Buddha nature, the Tao, the Good, the Word, and many other names.

All these terms are names. They are not that single, absolute non-dual entity as such, but describe that entity for the purposes of the particular creed and belief system. The only way of comprehending this entity is to be at one with it. To become one with it entails renunciation of anything and everything else. This renunciation must include not only the body with its attendant sensory adjuncts (smelling, tasting, seeing, touching, and listening,) but also the emotions and the mind—often referred to as the subtle world as opposed to the gross world.

It is universally the case right across the realm of human spirituality that the key to what has just been said is to disassociate one's feeling of identification from one's mind. This is the crux of the matter. It is so easy to give credence to the desires and aversions, the likes and dislikes, the fears and prejudices, the predilections, the opinions and beliefs, and operate as if they are essentially what I am. But we have seen that this is far from being the case. All are capable of being placed under observation, and in that place where observation can take place, it is essential for the mind to be quiet. In that situation, it becomes apparent that whatever else "I am", it is none of the above.

Whilst consciousness, or awareness, is universal and undifferentiated, and therefore can be said to inhabit all of creation including the above examples, to comprehend the truth of what we are requires us to "dis-identify," or disassociate from the mind. The mind can then be put to its right and proper function, which is to garner and appraise information in creation and ensure that the physical world is set to operate as is intended and so ensure that the well-being of all is maximised. And in the restful state that naturally ensues, it can be a suitable recipient for whatever influences are to be availed from the spiritual world.

To realise that we are not the beings who think but the silent witnesses of those thoughts is the beginning of human liberty or freedom. It then becomes apparent that there is a conscious awareness which utterly transcends the day-to-day concerns of our lives, and the lives of those around us. That is not in any way to diminish the importance of such concerns. It simply places them in context and in effect allows the need of the moment not only to be clearly identified, but also to act to meet that need with the necessary alacrity, efficiency and focus—what we have described in chapter 10 as attention controlled.

And over and above all of that, it becomes apparent that there is a vast realm of consciousness and comprehension which transcends the world of mind, that is at peace, and always was at peace, and always will be. That vast realm is the truth about you, and the truth about me, and all of humankind. All we have to do is to get out of the way—to blow the dust off the lightbulb, or to let the clouds part so that the sun can shine its light.

And what then? Why, all the things that make life worth living can be realised, can be seen to exist and are known to comprise our birthright— beauty, love, joy, peace, contentedness, well-being, creativity, and the rest. And of even greater significance, there is the understanding that they originate from a wholly different place than the mind. The mind is then perceived to be what it is—an instrument. A very potent, fine, powerful instrument, but *not* what "I am". And, like all instruments, it needs to be looked after, to be used in the correct way, and to be laid to rest when it is not required.

In this way, rather than being overwhelmed by one's emotional state, one can identify and simply observe the emotional world and continue to operate as a fully functioning human being despite the "slings and arrows of outrageous fortune", as Shakespeare put it in Hamlet, without losing one's composure or well-being. This is the true meaning of presence. These fears and anxieties are *not* of the present. They are of the future or past. Bringing the mind under control brings us into the present moment. And in the present moment things are quite simply not as the unbridled mind assumes them to be. Just consider—no matter how bad the debt, how awful the grief, how dire the divorce or break up, can you define what actual problem do you actually have now? Not next year, next week, in five minutes' time but *now*?

Meditation

To enter this desirable and blissful state of disassociation from the subtle world is where meditation comes in. Meditation is said by that great seer and teacher Shantananda Saraswati to comprise "the most important factor of development, which is the Meditation. This is the master key to all measures and full realisation".

Meditation is a thread which runs right through the great world non-dual teachings. Full realisation of the being requires full and regular practice of meditation. Now this is not something which is easily availed, because despite the plethora of meditation types, practices, and techniques, it is so easy so embark upon such a course full of enthusiasm only to be disappointed too quickly and then to drop out of the practice.

I will be outlining a number of meditative exercises later, and these can be practiced alone and at will, but there is no substitute for selecting a meditation style and technique which ideally needs to be taught by a trained initiate or expert, which can be monitored, and where back up and encouragement can be availed. Fortunately, there are today many schools, spiritual organisations, and other establishments where these attributes can be availed, some details of those that I have come across being detailed at the end of the book.[2] There will doubtless be many others, and the reader is recommended to make his or her own enquiries in this regard.

It has always been said that when the disciple is ready, the master appears. I cannot emphasise too firmly that the proper study of mindful philosophy, dealing as it does with the world of spirituality, requires time and commitment. This has got to be the inevitable situation if we are dealing with the highest aims of human life, to achieve full Self-knowledge, gnosis, or realisation. The need to practice meditation in a regular and disciplined manner is said by teachers such as Shantananda Saraswati to be of the very highest importance.

Meditation is essentially a technique involving turning inwards to still the mind. Many of the most popular types of meditation finding favour today involve the inward repetition of a sound, or word, called a *mantra*. The idea is for this sound, which in some traditions carries much spiritual energy or vibration, to form the subject of attention to replace what otherwise would be the mind not fully controlled, and so entering a depth of experience that is well beyond the day-to-day norm. This is the case with the transcendental meditation, which was introduced to the West in 1957 by the Maharishi Mahesh Yogi, who emanated from the same tradition as Shantananda Saraswati. To gain access to this technique requires tuition and initiation to ensure the practice starts in the most auspicious and beneficial manner. Initially, two periods per day of just 10-15 minutes are recommended. As the practice settles down and becomes established as an important part of the life, these timings can rise to two periods of 30 minutes.

A similar mantra-based technique is used within the Christian meditation tradition, in which there is also the idea of *contemplation*, which can be likened to some contemporary ideas of meditation. Meditation forms part of the core practices of Buddhism (dhyana), Zen (Zazen) and of Sufiism (Dhikr), the Kabbalah from the Jewish tradition, and as noted earlier, Hesychasm which is another Christian derivative from the Orthodox church.

There are in addition many mindfulness-based meditation practices, including focussing on the breathing. These are outlined on the CD which accompanies *Mindfulness: A Practical Guide* by Williams/Penman I have referred to above. Here again, it is far preferable to attend a mindfulness course than to simply rely upon books, no matter how valuable they may be. Some care is needed—some techniques of meditation are designed to assist the process of full spiritual realisation of the human being, whilst others are more modest in aspiration, intended just to help one feel a little better and brighter for a while. It is the former that is being recommended here, although the latter can be a very useful introduction. This is where the guidance of a school or teacher is most useful.

The benefits of meditation are not only the means whereby humankind can access freedom and realisation, albeit for the purposes of this book these remain the most significant attributes. Hardly a week passes without some reference in the mass media to a new study or research project proving the benefits to health and well-being from the practice of meditation. These range from stress and pain reduction to benefits to blood pressure, metabolism and the like.

I understand that a study by the US government in 2007 revealed that over 20 million adults in the United States had practiced meditation that year. Apparently, the figure continues to rise. In the UK in London, researches confirmed that the basal metabolic rate decreased by up to 40 per cent, and states of very deep repose were registered in the meditators. And these were followed up by heightened speeds of reaction during the post meditation period.

Also, it has been proven that meditation is a means whereby use of the right side of the brain, which is conducive to creativity, intuitive faculties and sensitivity is enhanced to reduce that very common Western issue of too much domination by the left side, which is more conducive to stress, to analysis, comparison and perpetually commentating. It is well known that the result of the meditative process leads to peace, serenity, well-being, calmness, space, and steadiness.

Shantananda Saraswati has succinctly outlined ten benefits or symptoms which will arise to those who regularly meditate using the mantra system:

- Improvements to physical health, and quicker recovery from sickness
- A sense of renunciation of useless things
- A proper sense of proportion in life (including being able to do what is needed and not doing what is not required due to excess uncurbed energy)
- Strengthening of our faculties of experience (including use of the five senses and the five organs of action)
- Increase in kindness and compassion, including the ability to forgive and to exercise enhanced mind control
- Loss of the sense of separation, including the idea of "me and mine"
- Freedom from greed, envy, and malice

- Freedom from fear

- Increase in self-confidence

- Increase in positiveness/reduction of gloominess

So to progress matters, I suggest that reference be made to the organisations outlined in *Being Oneself*.[3] Or if you have a particular allegiance to a specific tradition, see if there is a mystical side in which meditation is offered and give that high priority. Practicing within the context of a group of like-minded seekers is very beneficial and more powerful than relying upon one's own, and will give support and reassurance. Practicing at regular times of day, so that the practice can be assimilated and integrated into the life, is important. It needs a high priority.

Whatever type of meditation practice is embarked upon, there is a posture which would be helpful to allow the subtle energies to travel up the spinal column to where needed. The crucial point is for the back to be straight. This normally means sitting on a standard chair (no armchairs or soft furnishings) with limbs at right angles, back held straight and not resting on the back of the chair, the head held up so that if the eyes were open they would give a level gaze.

In this manner, it is almost as if there is a straight line from the head, through the neck and spine, to the seat. It is important not to allow a sag of the midriff. This can be difficult at first, but once this posture is achieved, the body seems perfectly balanced and stress-free. If there is back pain, then resting the back with cushions, or lying down, would be acceptable, provided that the spine is straight. The shoulders should relax, and any unnecessary tensions allowed to pass. The hands can be rested on the lap or gently clasped.

And, most importantly, going into a period of meditation, take the attitude that meditation is like greeting an old and much revered friend. Welcome it, and adopt the attitude that it really is now a very important facet of your life, and that whatever happens the practice will receive your highest priority and commitment.

For further information, a London-based organisation known as the School of Meditation has produced an admirable book on mantra meditation called *Being Oneself.*[4] This is an excellent manner in which to close with the facts, benefits, and practice of meditation, and I thoroughly recommend it.

Meditative and Mindful Practices

I am now going to outline some day-to-day practices which can be used as part and parcel of ordinary living. Again, the supportive encouragement of a group is most helpful, but I suggest these practices be experimented with at one's leisure.

Breathing

Those who have pursued the study of mindfulness via the various courses that are now available will be familiar with using breathing as a focus to still the mind, and that again is something that is of universal acknowledgement. One just notes, without commentary, the passage of air into, and then out of, the nose. One can note similarly the slight rise and fall of the diaphragm as this takes place. Likewise, the still point where the in breath becomes the out breath, and vice versa. One cannot attend to the breathing other than by being present, and therein lies the power of this simple but transformative exercise. In the fullness of time you will find that thoughts will enter and deflect the attention from the breathing. Well, never mind. Once one realises that, one simply reverts to the breathing without any commentary whatsoever. Practice in this way for five to ten minutes.

The Senses

Attention upon the senses is another area for mindful study. There are quite a number of mindful exercises, including the "chocolate" and "raisin" exercises, designed to refine our approach to taste, smell, touch—with other benefits. I outline hereunder an "awareness exercise" which encompasses these, and which can be expanded to allow observation of the subtle world as well. Adopting the posture outlined earlier, follow the procedure outlined thus:

- Sit in a comfortable yet balanced upright position as above outlined, with both feet on the ground.

- Feel the body—its weight on the chair, the feet upon the floor, the air flowing around the face, hands and neck.

- Feel the gentle pressure of the clothes upon the skin.

- Now bring the whole body into view, as it were, and be aware of the energy it contains, notably at the toes and fingers.

- Be aware of the senses—taste, smell, touch. Be in touch.

- If the eyes are open, note light, form, shape but without any commentary, and without going out to any specific form. If the eyes are shut, just note light.

- Listening—note sounds close by in the room. Note further sounds in the building itself. Now let the attention widen to include sounds outside. And now widening still further to the farthest sound. And beyond even that to, as it were, the silence beyond all sound, out of which the sound emanates.

- Simply rest in that silence, without commentary. After a while, thoughts will enter. As that happens, simply withdraw the attention from the thought, returning to the listening. In other words, don't energise the thought with the fuel of your attention but simply let it come to pass without commentary. Continue to rest for a few moments.

Another exercise using the senses is to allow, say, 20-30 minutes in which to take a walk. Divide the available time into three, and use a third each for attention on the senses of touch, of sight, and of listening. Try not to comment as this takes place. If in a group format, there could be a "report back" as to what was experienced—what happened to the mind, any sense of expansion, whether the exercise shone any light as to what *"I am"* in the process of placing creation under observation, and the like.

Insight Meditation

This is a similar exercise, designed to understand the nature of what is taking place in both the material and subtle (mental) worlds, by placing each movement or occurrence, under observation. By so doing, one becomes convinced of the impermanence, or transitory nature of each occurrence, whether physical or subtle. This process is said to ultimately lead the aspirant to a place of supreme tranquillity, brought about by the use of attention.

As one practices, one notes that whatever arises passes away after a while. One can then comprehend that these phenomena which come and go, in and out of our awareness, are but ephemeral manifestations—not the threatening and fear—inducing ogres that they can seem to be under more "normal" circumstances. It is understood that no phenomenon lasts forever. Here is the technique:

- Start by falling quite still. Note, as above, the simple fact that with every breath there is the rise, then fall, of the abdomen, rising as one inhales and falling as one exhales. Just note "rising", "falling" while continuing to breathe normally.

- As one proceeds, thoughts will enter the mind. Again, just note them similarly. If one becomes aware that the mind is wandering, simply note "wandering, wandering". If one starts to imagine, when one becomes aware of that simply note "imagining, imagining". If one finds oneself becoming happy, or bored, or disheartened, or whatever, just note "happy, bored, disheartened" as the case may be.

- In the same way, one will probably find that all manner of objects from the world of the senses will make their presence felt. As they do so, and as one becomes aware of that fact, simply note by way of observation in a disinterested manner "touching, touching, seeing, seeing, hearing, hearing" and so on.

At this stage, if time permits, one can go on a reflective walk for, say, 10 minutes. One can proceed here in the same vein, simply noting without commentary whatever the attention rests upon. This could include what has just been outlined, or it could include the actual act of walking (e.g., foot raised, pushed forward, foot lowered). One walks simply noting "raising, pushing forward, lowering". Again, if within a group context, this process can be followed up with a "report back" to share what has been seen and experienced. The point is just to observe. No commentary, judgement, analysis or appraisal is required. There is no success, and no failure, because there is no endeavour to seek any particular result. There is no such thing as a "good" or "bad" thought—by simply allowing the observation to function in an untrammelled way, a thought is understood to just be a thought—no more and no less.

Self-Enquiry

There are various exercises to continue with examination of what is real, or Self, as opposed to what is not real, or not—self. Here is a good example:

- Consider the physical body, which exists in the gross world, the world of form. Note how it occupies space and changes over time. Is that what "I" am?
- Observe the senses, and the sensations they produce:
  - o Touch—feel the clothes on the skin, the feet on the floor.
  - o Sight—allow colour and form to be observed without comment.
  - o Smell.
  - o Taste.
  - o Listen—allow the listening to be wide and all-embracing.

  Are these what "I" am?
- Emotions
  - o Reflect upon the ever changing emotions—anger, pain, anguish, grief, pleasure.

  Are these what "I" am?

- Thoughts
    - o Be aware of thoughts—whether they are beliefs, opinions, wishes, desires, goals, aversions.
    - o Are they subject to change?

  Are these what "I" am?

- The Observer
    - o What is it that observes our ordinary mental and emotional experiences, and the ceaselessly changing worlds of body and mind?
    - o Is there something which is still, which itself does *not* change?
    - o What is it that is observing here and now?

  Is this what "I" am?

- With body and mind at rest, continue to rest in the peace of yourSelf for a few minutes.

Presence

Slowly read the following passage and then spend a few minutes quietly resting in the peace of yourSelf:

> What is my life for me now? What am I? Who am I?
>
> I am being. I am consciousness. I am perfect bliss.

I am one with all. I am one with creation in all its fullness, and in each and every part.

I am one with the element earth, with its fragrance and its ability to bring forth the life of seeds and plants.

I am one with the element water, the rains, the rivers, the oceans, and its ability to bring forth taste.

I am one with fire, and its capacity to enlighten, to heat, to burn, and its ability to bring forth sight.

I am one with air, the breath of life, its ability to support and touch. I am in touch.

I am one with space in its vastness, and its ability to conduct sound and enable listening.

I am one with the whole of the manifest creation, the world of nature, the creatures of the earth and all that lives thereon.

I am one with the whole of humanity. There is no separation.

I am one with the universe—the "one song". There is no separation.

I am being. I am consciousness. I am perfect Bliss. I know this to be so because I am present, here, now.

TO CONCLUDE

There are a number of areas in which a "ladder" of progress can be discerned. This is a notion which needs to be used with some care, as the true Self needs no ladder, any more than it did a gate, or a house in Baghdad containing treasure which featured in our earlier examples. But we are where we are, and it is useful to see how we can in some way measure up to the spiritual pathway. I set out under such a ladder, as outlined by one Dr Francis C. Roles, who led another UK-based organisation in taking instruction on the subject of non-duality or *Advaita* philosophy from Sri Shantananda Saraswati, known as the Study Society, or the Society for the Study of Normal Psychology, as referred to in the bibliography under chapter 1. This example can be found with other detail of the type in the succinct and eminently accessible book, *Being: The Teaching of Advaita, A Basic Introduction* by Philip Jacobs.[5]

1) GOOD ACTIONS: with attention, "worthy of the supreme Self".
2) GOOD THOUGHTS: benevolence, cheerful attitude.
3) DECREASE OF BAD THOUGHTS: ill will, criticism, grumbling.
4) SATTVA (peace, light, stillness) begins to dominate.
5) DECREASE IN POWER OVER US OF WORDLY ATTRACTIONS: less identification.
6) GIVING UP WORDLY OBJECTIVES: (i.e. ambitions, dropping out of the rat race, but observing one's duties and obligations).

7) LIBERATION FROM ALL THOUGHTS ABOUT ONESELF:

and one's profit and loss.

Dr Roles continues:

> It must be remembered that these are not rigid steps, that their characteristics are all potentially present in each of us, for the Atman (Big I, Self) is present in us, though not realised by us owing to the cloud of ignorance that surrounds Him. Consequently each day we probably have experiences for moments of at least six of these steps, our task being to make them more and more permanent in us. I have to start each day with the first step, and often several times in the day, but I try never to stay on that first step for long.

So, there is another practical exercise we might care to experiment with.

Now that we have taken a good, long and hard look at this idea of "mindful philosophy", perhaps we can finish with a brief resume of the salient points about this idea and how it relates to us. I set out a few briefly outlined summaries:

- I am not this ephemeral, unpredictable being with a name and a form. I am the one Self, and am therefore Divine, beyond birth and death, and immortal.
- I am being, truth, consciousness, and bliss.

- I am transcendent beyond anything that is created, yet immanent within all of it.

- I am a universal being shining in an individual body/mind.

- I am at my happiest when universal values such as love, brotherhood, compassion, and courage are allowed to prevail over individual values that relate to "me and mine".

- True wisdom is universal, practical, and truthful. It has nothing to do with the garnering of information for its own sake.

- To be truly happy means to live in the present moment.

- To live in the present moment means to rise beyond the contents of the mind, and thereby dissociate from it.

- In truth, nothing can harm me.

- If attention is in place, work ceases to be drudgery and becomes a vehicle for love to flow.

- There is continual amazement at the beauty of creation, and gratitude that there is no separation between me and whoever/ whatever produced this wondrous universe.

May every blessing shine upon you in your study and practice of non-duality, or mindful philosophy.

ABOUT THE BOOK

We are going to take something of a rollercoaster ride in our quest for self-discovery. In our peregrinations, we will be considering, first, what is this idea of mindful philosophy and, second, why it might be important in the twenty-first century in which there appears to be something of a spiritual reappraisal taking place.

NOTES

Chapter 1

[1]   Aldous Huxley, *The Perennial Philosophy* (1945). This book provides a detailed investigation of unitive teachings with a comprehensive range of quotations from many sources. It outlines the basic principles of the perennial philosophy in a somewhat different format, which I have adopted in chapter 8.

[2]   Jon Kabat-Zinn has produced many books, articles, and talks on mindfulness, and the reader interested in following this up is recommended to start with the internet, where the full range can be availed. Many authorities would consider him to be the leading authority in modern mindfulness and its teaching.

[3]   The book by Mark Williams and Danny Penman entitled *Mindfulness: A Practical Guide to Finding Peace in a Frantic World* (Piatkus, 2011) contains an eight-week programme in mindfulness, with CD accompaniment, as well as a wealth of background information and illustrations.

[4]   Thich Nhat Hanh, *Going Home: Jesus and Buddha as Brothers* (Rider, 1999). Thich Nhat Hanh has produced many works on Mindfulness, including *The*

Miracle of Mindfulness (Rider, 2008). They are succinct, easy to read, and provide a necessary degree of spirituality to illuminate what is often perceived as a subject limited to the world of therapy and self-help.

Chapter 2

[1]   Shanti Sadan and the School of Economic Science are both London-based charitable organisations offering instruction in non-dual philosophy with an Advaita-based stance. The latter is a worldwide organization, offering courses in what is described mainly as practical philosophy throughout its many centres. I can highly recommend these courses to the mindful philosophy seeker (go to www.philosophyworks.org if using the internet) because they comprise groups of like-minded and supportive seekers, and introduce meditation with a backup arrangement for their attendees. Shanti Sadan offers a most useful quarterly publication, *Self Knowledge*, which I commend to the mindful philosophy student.

[2]   Paul Brunton, *Inner Reality* (1945).

[3]   Juliet Mabey, *Rumi: A Spiritual Treasury* (Oneworld, 2000).

[4]   Darryl Reanney, *Music of the Mind* (Souvenir Press, 1988).

Chapter 3

[i]   Gospel of St Thomas. There are various editions, and I have used that compiled by Hugh McGregor Ross (Element Books, 1987).

ii)   Richard Rohr, from "What is the False Self?"—Daily Meditation 2017. This American author has also issued books such as *Falling Upwards* (SPCK, 2012) which is most useful.

iii) The World Community for Christian Meditation is the body governing the mantra-based meditation espoused by John Main and Fr. Lawrence Freeman, whose output should be considered by the mindful philosophy student with a Christian-based background. I can also recommend in this regard *Mindfulness and Christian Spirituality* by Tim Stead (SPCK, 2016).

iv)   Bede Griffiths was a Benedictine monk who embraced Advaita Vedanta, this union being the inspiration of a number of books, including *The Universal Christ* (Darton, Longman, and Todd, 1990). Also recommended are *The Marriage of East and West* (Collins, 1982) and *Vedanta and Christian Faith* (Dawn Horse Press, 1973).

v)   The letters of Marsilio Ficino are being translated and published by the School of Economic Science, the parent body of the Practical Philosophy Schools outlined above (Shepheard-Walwyn, 2003).

Chapter 4

1   Tobias Churton, *Gnostic Philosophy* (Inner Traditions, 2005).

2   The Nag Hammadi scrolls have been exhaustively appraised by a number of scholars, including Elaine Pagels, who produced a number of books on Gnosticism, including *The Gnostic Paul* (Fortress Press, 1975).

3   Freke and Gandy produced their book *The Jesus Mysteries* (Three Rivers Press, 1999) which draws attention to the Gnostic traditions, coming out of paganism, and evolving into a mystical interpretation of the Christian story integrating it with tales of other "God-men" including the Osiris/Isis allegory, and contrasting this with the Roman-instigated literalist interpretation, which ultimately and perforce triumphed over the Gnostic teaching.

4   Andrew Phillip Smith, *The Secret History of the Gnostics* and *The Lost Teachings of the Cathars* (Watkins, 2015).

5   A. P. Shepherd, *A Scientist of the Invisible* (Hodder and Stoughton Ltd, 1954).

6   Salaman, van Oyen, Wharton et al., *The Way of Hermes* (Duckworth, 1999).

7   Juliet Mabey, *Rumi: A Spiritual Treasury* (Oneworld Publications, 2000).

Chapter 5

1   Tim Freke, *The Mystery Experience* (Watkins, 2013).

2   Malcolm Hollick, *The Science of Oneness* (O-Books 2016).

Chapter 6

1   Sri Shantananda Saraswati, *Good Company* (The Society for the Study of Normal Psychology, 2009).

2   Sri Nisargadatta Maharaj, *I Am That: Talks with Sri Nisargadatta* (Sundaram Art Printing Press, 2009).

3   Eckhart Tolle, *Stillness Speaks* (Hodder and Stoughton, 2003).

4   Juan Mascaro, *Lamps of Fire* (Methuen, 1961).

5   Swami Sunirmalananda, *Insights into Vedanta—Tattwabodha* (Sri Ramakrishna Math Printing Press, 2005).

6   Adi Shankara, *Crest Jewel of Discrimination*, translated Swami Prabhavananda/Isherwood.

Chapter 7

1   Archbishop Desmond Tutu, *God Has a Dream* (Doubleday, 2004).

2   Tutu, *God Has a Dream*.

3   From a letter in 1855 from the chief of the Seattle Tribe in response to a request from President Franklin Pierce.

4   Ann Gadd, *Climbing the Beanstalk* (Findhorn Press, 2007).

Chapter 8

1   Ken Wilber, *The Eye of the Spirit* (Shambala, 2001).

2   *Collected Works of Ramana Maharshi*, ed. Arthur Osborne (Rider & Co, 1959).

3   R. W. Emerson, from first series of essays, 1841.

4   James Allen, *As a Man Thinketh* (1903).

5   Allen, *As a Man Thinketh*.

6   Richard Jefferies, *The Story of my Heart* (Longmans, 1883).

7   *Truth Is a Pathless Land* (The Krishnamurti Foundation America).

8   *Truth Is a Pathless Land*.

9   St Augustine of Hippo, *The Retractions*.

10   *The Collected Works of Ramana Maharshi*, edited by Arthur Osborne.

11   *The Collected Works of Ramana Maharshi*.

12   Deepak Chopra, *The Seven Laws of Spiritual Success* (Bantam Press, 2006).

13   Ken Wilber, *Theory of Everything* (Gateway, 2001).

14   Ken Wilber, *No Boundary* (Shambala, 2001).

Chapter 9

1   Werner Heisenberg, *Scientific and Religious Truth* (1974).

2   Alfred Einstein, "On Human Beings" (1954).

3   Rupert Sheldrake, *The Science Delusion* (Coronet, 2012).

4   Quoted verbally from Edgar Mitchell whilst on board Apollo 14.

5   Lynne McTaggart, *The Field* (Element/Harper Collins, 2003).

6   Dr Bruce Lipton, *The Biology of Belief* (Hay House, 2005).

7   F. David Peat, *Infinite Potential: The Life and Times of David Bohm* (1997).

Chapter 10

1   Nisargadatta Maharaj, *I Am That*.

2   Maharaj, *I Am That*.

3   From the forward to *Mindfulness: A Practical Guide to Finding Peace in a Frantic World*.

4   Vivekananda, *Work and its Secret* (Advaita Ashrama 2015).

5   A similar tale is to be found in the well-known and highly recommended book by Robert Holden *Happiness Now* (Hay House, 1998). I suggest that this readable and entertaining book is an excellent introduction to the principles underlying non-duality.

6   *The Power of Now* (Hodder and Stoughton, 1999) together with its compatriots, *A New Earth* (Penguin 2005), *Practicing the Power of Now* (Hodder and Stoughton 1992), and *Stillness Speaks* (Hodder and Stoughton 2003) by Eckhart Tolle are a first-class, highly lucid, and practical group of books which speak with authority and clarity on the subject matter of this book.

Chapter 11

1   This is from a publication called "A Book of Words" and was given by Kipling at a dinner speech in 1923.

2   The Schools of Practical Philosophy as mentioned at chapter 2 above offer courses in preparation for the introduction of mantra meditation. These are available throughout the English speaking world. See website as outlined above.

The School of Meditation is the body responsible for arranging initiations to this type of meditation—go to www.schoolofmeditation.org

The transcendental movement is another direction one can take—www. TM.org, or try www.davidlynchfoundation.org

Also recommended is the Study Society, or the Society for the Study of Normal Psychology. www.studysociety.org.

The world council for Christian meditation offer full details about meditation within a Christian context - wccm.org or wccm-usa.org.

3   *Being Oneself* (Biddles Ltd, 1985).

4   *Being Oneself.*

5   Philip Jacobs, *Being: The Teaching of Advaita, A Basic Introduction* (The Study Society, 2007).

ABOUT THE AUTHOR

Michael Snow has studied and practiced mindful philosophy, or the philosophy of non duality, for over 30 years, and has tutored them for 20. His interest in the subject evolved from his childhood experiences as a boy chorister at the great cathedral of Ely, which provided both a spiritual and an aesthetic grounding to set a direction of travel for his life path. Spirituality is the essential focus of his interest. His studies have brought him to the view that this can be undertaken in a non – religious or secular manner, and that underpinning all religions lies a unitive or non – dual essence that can be realized by anyone so moved, irrespective of religion or culture. He has investigated the question of sound, music and how modern science and the mystical traditions of old seem to share a common platform here. Michael now gives talks and holds discussions on these subjects, and writes articles for magazines and other publications. He has been practicing meditation since 1968, and believes that this is the key area for those interested in mindful philosophy to investigate. He is a member of the School of Economic Science where he studies and tutors.